M000114939

Mr. Snow's Magical Christmas

LAURA STEPHENS COLE

Copyright © 2021 Laura Stephens Cole.

All rights reserved. No part of this book may be used or reproduced by any means, graphic, electronic, or mechanical, including photocopying, recording, taping or by any information storage retrieval system without the written permission of the author except in the case of brief quotations embodied in critical articles and reviews.

LifeRich Publishing is a registered trademark of The Reader's Digest Association, Inc.

LifeRich Publishing books may be ordered through booksellers or by contacting:

LifeRich Publishing
1663 Liberty Drive
Bloomington, IN 47403
www.liferichpublishing.com
844-686-9607

Because of the dynamic nature of the Internet, any web addresses or links contained in this book may have changed since publication and may no longer be valid. The views expressed in this work are solely those of the author and do not necessarily reflect the views of the publisher, and the publisher hereby disclaims any responsibility for them.

Any people depicted in stock imagery provided by Getty Images are models, and such images are being used for illustrative purposes only. Certain stock imagery © Getty Images.

ISBN: 978-1-4897-3187-6 (sc)
ISBN: 978-1-4897-3188-3 (hc)
ISBN: 978-1-4897-3343-6 (e)

Library of Congress Control Number: 2021900943

Print information available on the last page.

LifeRich Publishing rev. date: 09/13/2021

I dedicate this book to my four beloved children who were the inspiration that went into this story. Each year I look forward to more surprises, traditions and memories we treasure together. Mom, thanks for the continuous encouragement and love. To all my special family and friends, thank you for all the unwavering support.

CHAPTER 1

Far away in a magical place lived a chubby, jolly snowman named Mr. Snow. He lived in an ice-covered cabin right next door to his best friend, Santa Claus. With more and more children being born all around the world, it was difficult for Santa to keep up with all the Christmas lists. So around the Christmas holiday, Mr. Snow did what he could to help Santa out. This year Santa hired several new elves to help with the busy holiday rush and to finish on time.

"Good morning, Santa! I'm here bright and early to help with the toys. What can I do first?" Mr. Snow merrily slid into the toy factory. He peeked around to see what had been completed and saw the elves busy hammering, assembling, painting, and wrapping gifts for the good little boys and girls to open on Christmas morning.

"Mr. Snow, you look tired. Are you feeling well?" Santa asked with concern.

"Sure. I'm as fit as a Christmas fiddle, Santa."

"Are you sure?"

"Actually, other than feeling a little bit tired, I've never felt better," Mr. Snow said.

"Is that all? Could I trust you to tell me if there were anything else bothering you?"

"I certainly would, Santa. Have you ever known me to keep a secret from my very best friend?"

"Well no, but I do know you've been extremely busy lately with work and all the extra things you've been doing to help Mrs. Claus in her shop. Anyway, I've hired a couple of elves this year to help me finish on time. Since you've helped me prepare for Christmas for so many years, why don't you take this year off?" said Santa.

"Well, I have been thinking about catching up on my rest. All right. It sounds like a great idea," Mr. Snow said.

So with Christmas drawing nearer, Mr. Snow decided a change of scenery would be nice. With his trusty sleigh—which he named Wonder Sleigh—and his cane, he set off in search of a nice quiet place to stay until Christmas passed.

CHAPTER 2

As MR. SNOW GLIDED ALONG, he wound through a mountain range and happened upon a small, snow-capped cottage nestled in the woods. It looked cozy and inviting. As he gazed upon it, he noticed it overlooked an ice-covered pond. All at once, a car barreled up the driveway and headed straight toward him. Quickly, he glided out of the way just in time.

"Wow. She drives her car like Santa drives his sleigh," Mr. Snow said softly.

The driver came to an abrupt halt and jumped out of the car to apologize to him. She was an older lady wearing a long white coat and a matching blue knitted hat and pair of gloves. Quickly, she walked over to where he was still standing on the sleigh.

"Goodness me! I'm so sorry! I almost hit you. Are you all right?" the woman asked nervously.

"You didn't hurt me one bit, ma'am. I'm as fit as a fiddle." He bent down to pick up his hat and glasses.

"I'm very happy to hear that." She sighed in relief.

"Hello! My name is Mr. Snow." He reached out his hand to give her a warm handshake.

"Oh, hi. I'm Caroline." She smiled and removed her gloves to shake his hand. "I don't normally drive so fast, but I've been so busy with Christmas coming in a few days. I have been planning a party for Christmas Eve, as well as getting ready for the holiday. I seem to have misplaced my glasses. Without them, I can't see my hand in front of my face." She laughed.

"I know exactly what you are talking about, Caroline. I live at the North Pole, right next door to my best friend. You could call me his right-hand snowman."

They both chuckled.

"Anyway, each year I help the big guy in his workshop. It does get very busy, but please don't tell anyone. It's a secret." Mr. Snow laughed.

"I'm sure it would be overwhelming to have such an important job! Please excuse me for asking, Mr. Snow, but why aren't you helping out this year?"

"It's funny you should ask that. You see, Santa gave me this year off. He said I needed some time to rest until after the rush is over. So as I was gliding along, I came upon your home and stopped to admire how beautiful it is."

"Mr. Snow, would you like to spend your vacation here?" Caroline graciously offered.

"That would be splendid, madam! Thank you so much." He smiled.

CHAPTER 3

MR. SNOW MADE HIMSELF AT home. He began to see all the things he had been too busy to admire before. The ice on the pond glistened as the ducks glided across it. The fields were covered in a blanket of sparkling snow. He watched as the cows ate fresh hay. The birds in the trees sang a glorious song. They were waiting for spring to arrive, when they would take flight and enjoy all the wonders of the world.

Then Mr. Snow's thoughts drifted back to all the Christmases filled with treasured memories of his loving family and dearest friends. He missed them and wished they were there with him to enjoy such pleasures. He realized it would not be long before he saw them all again. And when he did, he would tell them about his adventure, everything he got to enjoy, and the new friends he made.

That evening, while he was enjoying a lovely moonlit night, the sky filled with bright stars. Mr. Snow fell soundly asleep. But he was abruptly awakened by the worst winds he had ever felt.

"Oh my! What is a snowman to do with such fierce winds?" he said to himself.

He remembered Caroline had told him that if he needed anything to let her know. Mr. Snow slid quickly over to her bedroom window, peeked through the curtains, and rapidly knocked. He got no response. He knocked again even louder.

"Caroline! Oh, Caroline! Hellooooooooooooooooo! Hey, you next to

Caroline, please wake up!" There was no way and no how they could possibly hear him with all that snoring.

Suddenly, a strong gust of wind came whipping by and was about to take him for a ride. Luckily, he grabbed onto a tree with both hands. He held on with all his might and hoped the fierce winds would die down soon. Instead, the winds continued to blow with more intensity.

"*Oh no!*" he screamed.

The wind started pulling Mr. Snow's body apart. His hand-knitted scarf and glasses were the first to blow away. Then he lost his grip and his arms went sailing through the air. Mr. Snow's body was like a kite going up, up, and up. He landed headfirst in a huge pile of snow.

"Woe is me," he moaned. "I won't budge an inch from this spot until the wind dies down."

"Good gracious! I've never seen anything like that before," snipped a small dog with an English accent.

"Hello there, little fellow. What is your name?" Mr. Snow asked as the little dog walked toward him wagging his tail.

"My name is Brutus. You are a dirty creature. How about I clean you up a bit?" Brutus asked and began to lick Mr. Snow's dirty face.

"Oh no! Stop it! That is my tickle spot. Not there. Oh, not there!" Mr. Snow said as he laughed.

Brutus paid no attention to Mr. Snow and continued cleaning him off.

"You need to go play. I can't handle too much more of this." Mr. Snow chuckled.

"Pip-pip and cheerio to you then, you strange looking creature," Brutus said. He stuck his nose up, turned around, and trotted away.

CHAPTER 4

WHEN MORNING FINALLY ARRIVED, IT brought a welcome relief from the fierce winds. Caroline was leaving to pick up some last-minute party favors and Christmas gifts. Walking toward her car, she noticed Mr. Snow lying in a big pile of snow.

"My goodness, what happened to you Mr. Snow?" she asked. She dropped her purse and hurried over to where he lay.

"Caroline, is that you?" Mr. Snow said while trying to look around.

"Yes, it is. What happened to you?"

"There was a strong wind last night. It almost blew me back home! I feel like I was used in a snowball fight and lost. Just look at me. I'm a mess."

"I would love to help you get up, but you have no arms."

"Yes, I know. I've been doing a lot of thinking. I thought if I could roll over, I could loosen the snow around me. Then maybe you can give me a big push so I can stand up." He wiggled and grunted, twisted and turned, and finally got himself loose enough for her to push him up. "OK, I'm ready ... One, two, three," shouted Mr. Snow as Caroline pushed.

"Ah, there we go. Good as new!" Caroline said. She began pulling some sticks out of his body.

"Well, almost as good as new. As you can see, I'm short a few things. What in the name of the North Pole am I supposed to do now? I don't feel like a complete snowman. There is no way I can go home looking like this." He looked down at his body.

7

"Mr. Snow, please don't get upset. I am sure the rest of you is somewhere around here." Caroline began looking around to see if she could find anything that belonged to him. "I would be delighted to help you look, but I'm in such a big hurry. I still have so much to do before the party. I'm so sorry Mr. Snow," she said sadly.

"I understand completely," he said. He dropped his head and began to cry.

"Wait a minute. I have a wonderful idea! Why didn't I think of this sooner? Whatever you are unable to locate today, we will have the children who are coming to the party help you find."

"Would they? You don't think they would mind helping out an old snowman, do you?"

"Not at all! They are sweet children." She smiled. "Well, I have got to run, but I will catch up with you when I return. Please help yourself to anything you need," she said. She started walking quickly to her car.

"Please drive carefully!" Mr. Snow shouted.

"I will try and watch for snowmen along the way," she said, laughing. She jumped in her car and sped off.

CHAPTER 5

A DAY HAD PASSED, AND MR. Snow was still unable to find any of his missing parts. That was OK, though, because he knew the children would be there soon to help him. He was so excited to meet all the boys and girls Caroline had spoken of. He had a special place in his heart for children. The party was planned for that afternoon, and people were coming and going all morning. Some were staying for the party, and others were dropping their children off.

"I can't understand it. No one has stopped to help me or even just say hello," Mr. Snow said softly.

He slid over to the window and peeked in. They were having such a fun time laughing, singing, playing, and enjoying the wonderful Christmas party.

Mr. Snow began to think of his friends at the North Pole and how he wished he had never left. Suddenly the front door flew open and hit the house with a loud bang. The boys and girls ran over to him with such energy. They all had big smiles on their faces.

"Hello, boys and girls. My name is—" he began.

"We know who you are," said a little girl named Emily, giggling.

A little boy chimed in. "These are my sisters, Shelby, Sarah, and Emily, and I'm Jeremy. Grandma told us all about you."

"Yes. We also know all about your little problem too, don't we children?" Caroline asked as she peeked out from behind the children.

"Oh hi, Caroline. I was beginning to think you had forgotten all about me," he said.

"No matter how busy things get with the holiday, I could never forget about you." Caroline smiled.

"It looks like we have a lot of work to do," another little boy said.

"Jonathan and Katie are two more of my grandchildren. They are also brother and sister."

"Mr. Snow, did you almost blow away like a balloon?" Katie asked.

"I sure did, sweetie." He leaned over to look into her blue eyes and asked, "Are you sure it won't be too much work for you? You will miss your party."

"We don't mind at all, and besides, we don't need a Christmas party. I would much rather help you," Jonathan said.

"Instead of a Christmas party, we will have a treasure hunting party," Shelby added.

"Sounds snowsational." Mr. Snow chuckled. He looked around at all their bright, shiny faces and then at Caroline. "You were right Caroline, they are very sweet children."

"Thank you," all the children said.

"You are welcome, but I do wish there were some way I could repay you for your generosity."

"I'm sure something will come up. Right, children?" Caroline asked.

"Yes!" they said.

"Where should we begin?" Mr. Snow asked.

"Why don't we split up into teams? That would be the quickest way to get the job done," Jeremy said. "Shelby, you come with me, and we will search around the pond. Emily and Sarah will check around the house, shed, and yard. Jonathan, since you are the oldest, why don't you and Katie check out the woods and fields?"

"I'm afraid I won't be much help," Mr. Snow said sadly.

"That's OK. We will look for you," Emily said as she put her arm around him.

"Let's meet back here in a couple of hours," Jonathan said.

"Great! Let's get going," Jeremy insisted.

"Make sure you all bundle up and be careful," Caroline said.

"Yeah. Uncle Kevin spotted a bear cub in the woods. Its mom should not be too far behind," Jonathan said.

"Maybe we better pass," Mr. Snow said, looking concerned.

"That was way back in the woods near an old creepy barn. The children will not be going back into the woods that deep," Caroline assured him.

"Are you sure?" Mr. Snow asked.

"I am positive. If I thought the children would be in any kind of danger, I would not let them go," she said.

"That's settled. Let's get going," Jeremy said.

"We have to hurry up so we can get into bed early. Otherwise, Santa won't come," Emily told the others.

As Caroline and Mr. Snow waved goodbye, the children set off on what they thought was going to be a quick trip. Little did they know, an adventure lay ahead.

CHAPTER 6

JEREMY AND SHELBY WERE THE first to head off.

"A-hunting we will go, a-hunting we will go. Heigh ho, to the pond, oh, a-hunting we will go," Shelby sang.

"You're too much." Jeremy laughed.

"Thank you, treasure hunter." She giggled.

"Shelby, it's a good thing we have our snow boots and earmuffs to keep us warm. Man, it's so cold!"

"It really is." She shivered.

A steady breeze blew as the snow fell like soft pieces of cotton. The air was cold and crisp. The shimmering pond looked like glass, and the trees were covered in a thin layer of snow. They looked like they had been dipped in powdered sugar.

"This is a perfect day," Shelby said. She looked at all the beautiful things around them. "I feel like singing another song, Jeremy."

"Oh no. Not another song. Could you not?" he demanded.

"Come on. Please," she asked.

"Well, I guess there is no way out of it. OK. That's fine."

"Mommy says I'm a great little singer."

"That's a matter of opinion." He laughed.

"We can both sing. After all, no one can hear us."

They began to sing "Jingle Bells," but as soon as they saw it, they quickly fell silent. Right in front of them stood the famous spooky covered bridge. It was the quickest way to the pond. It had been built years ago by an old man they named Grandpa Stephens. He was a carpenter and very talented. You could see the fine craftsmanship in everything he built, including the house Caroline called her retirement home.

The weather had taken its toll on the bridge, and it needed to be replaced. From time to time, they would hear the adults talking about the old bridge and how it wouldn't make it through another bad winter with heavy snow.

They stood and stared in silence, trying to decide if they should cross it or take the long way around. Despite their doubts, they decided to use it. As the wind blew, the bridge creaked and moaned like it was talking to them in a scary language of its own. They cautiously began to creep across it, trying not to make a sound. When they reached the other side, they were relieved that the bridge hadn't fallen down on them. They continued to sing where they had left off in the song, as if they were never interrupted. As they neared the pond, they heard a frantic quacking sound.

"It sounds like one of the ducks is in trouble," Jeremy said.

They started to run as fast as they could through the snow.

"Look, one of the baby ducks is stuck in the middle of the pond, and ice is all around it," he said.

"Its mommy is over there. How do you think it got over there?" Shelby asked.

"I don't know, but let's hurry up and save it," Jeremy said.

"Momma, where are you?" cried the baby duck.

"Momma is right here. I can't get through the ice to you. If my wing weren't hurt, I could fly over and save you. What happened?"

"Well, I was taking a nap like you told me to and all of a sudden something smacked my face. It made me fly in the air, and now I'm way over here."

"Somebody, help my baby!" the momma duck quacked frantically.

"Come on. Let's hurry and hop into the boat. It will be much faster," Jeremy said to Shelby

He and Shelby jumped in. He sat in the middle of the boat, grabbed the oars, pushed off the shore, and began to row.

"Grandma never uses this lots of fun boat," she said.

"I wonder why she doesn't. It looks like a perfectly good boat to me."

"Well, we've got it now," she said with a grin.

As Jeremy rowed through the thin layer of ice to the baby duck, he noticed water beginning to come into the bottom of the boat.

"Oh no. Now I know why Grandma doesn't use the boat. There is a leak in it," he said.

"What are we going to do now?" Shelby shouted.

"We are going to hurry up and rescue the duck and then get all of us back to shore as quickly as possible. Maybe the hole isn't that big. I hope."

"We're not going to make it back. The boat is going to sink!" Shelby yelled.

"No it's not. Everything is going to be OK."

"Did you forget that I can't swim?"

Jeremy started rowing as fast as he could, not letting his sister know how scared he was at possibly not making it back. They reached the baby duck in the nick of time. He looked worn out, and Jeremy wasn't sure how much longer he would have lasted.

Quickly reaching down, he scooped the duckling up and handed him to Shelby. She tucked him in her coat and completely forgot about the sinking boat.

"You poor baby. You must be so cold." She began to sing a soothing lullaby to relax him.

"What is that on your face little duck?" Jeremy asked.

Shelby started to laugh. "It's a pair of glasses. How do you suppose they got there?"

"Shelby, I bet they belong to Mr. Snow." Jeremy laughed.

"I betcha they are. I don't think this guy has been to the eye doctor lately. Let me help you, cute little quacker," she said as she removed the glasses and handed them to her brother.

He put them in his pocket for safe keeping until he could give them back to Mr. Snow. As soon as they reached the side of the pond, Jeremy grabbed Shelby's hand and they both jumped out. They watched as the boat sank. They took the baby duck over to his mom and set him down right next to her.

"Momma, Momma, I thought I'd never see you again. I love you so much, Momma."

"I love you too, son. It scares me to know that if these nice people hadn't come along, I may have never seen you again," she said as she wrapped her uninjured wing around him.

CHAPTER 7

Meanwhile, the others were headed out to begin their own searches.

"Come on, Katie. We need to hurry up. There is a large area to cover and very little time!" Jonathan said.

"I know, I know. Good grief, Jonathan. I'm going as fast as I can go," she replied.

"Why don't we check out the field where the cows are first?" he asked, and they headed toward the field.

New snow had fallen and covered the field that the children used for sledding and snowboarding. Not only did the children love coming to Grandma's during the winter to enjoy the rolling hills, but they also considered springtime a great time to play and run through the plush grass.

Across the field, the bulls and cows stood chewing the hay that had been given to them a little later than usual. It had been placed in piles all around for all to enjoy. The calves nuzzled against their mothers' warm bellies, getting their morning breakfast. In another field nearby, the horses were envious, for they had not yet received their hay and oats for the day.

"What is this thing on my head? Would somebody move it? I can't see how to eat," Herman the bull said. He tried shaking the item off his head.

His wife, Daisy May, said, "Settle down, dear. Whatever it is, maybe I can help you get it off. Just drop your head, and I'll kick it far away."

"What if you miss and kick me?"

"I will be careful and try not to harm you. Face it, Herman. You have no other choice. It's either let me try to remove it or walk around with that thing on your head all day long."

"I guess you are right. Here goes nothing," Herman said. He dropped his head and closed his eyes tightly.

"OK, Herman, here we go. Oh no. I can't. *Ugh*. I can't get my foot up high enough to reach. I'm so sorry, dear."

"Jonathan, I'm getting tired. Please wait," Katie hollered.

"I'm right at the gate, Katie. Come on. Catch up," he hollered back.

When he reached the gate, he realized that Katie had fallen behind and was out of sight. He climbed up onto the gate, sat down on the top, and waited for her to catch up. "Katie, watch out for the barbed wire. You could get hurt," he called.

"OK," she replied. "Look at the cows. Aren't they big?" she asked when she reached him. "What are we looking for anyway, Jonathan?

"I don't know, but I'm sure we will know when we find it."

"That one looks a little silly," Katie said as she pointed her small finger toward a group of cows eating.

"I think that bull is wearing a hat. How on earth do you think it got there, Katie?"

Giggling, she said, "I don't know, but I guarantee the hat belongs to Mr. Snow. I've never seen a bull wearing a hat before."

"Stay here while I get Mr. Snow's hat. He jumped down, opened the gate and then quickly closed it tightly behind him. Katie climbed up to watch. As Jonathan was walking toward the bull, he suddenly noticed another bull, much larger than the one wearing the hat. It stood alone in the corner of the field. The large bull stood with his massive horns pointing toward the ground and was digging his foot in the snow. Jonathan knew exactly what the bull was going to do.

"Katie, get off the gate. He's going to charge!" he yelled.

Cupping her hands around her mouth, Katie yelled at Jonathan. "Run fast!"

In spite of the massive bull charging, Jonathan kept running toward the bull wearing the hat.

"Jonathan, you're going the wrong way!"

"Just who do you think you are, coming into my pasture?" snorted the charging bull. "This is my domain and no one else's. If you don't want to leave, then I'll make you."

"Herman, what do you suppose that bull is doing?" Daisy May asked.

"Who knows and who cares what that crazy bull is up to. Ever since he got here, he thinks he owns the place," Herman replied.

"Quick, open the gate!" Jonathan yelled.

As soon as he slid through the gate, he slammed it shut. Seconds later, there was a tremendous thud as the angry bull slammed into the gate.

"*Whew*, that was close." Jonathan laughed as he wiped the sweat from his face.

"Were you scared?" Katie asked.

"No, not at all, sis. It was just like a run in the park. Ha ha. Were you too busy watching the bull to notice that I got Mr. Snow's hat back?"

CHAPTER 8

Emily AND SARAH WERE NOT sure where to begin their hunt.

"I have an idea. Why don't we hook Grandma's sleigh up to the dogs and ride around looking for parts to Mr. Snow?" Emily asked.

"That's a terrific idea. Sometimes you surprise me. You get the dogs, and I'll get the hot cocoa," Sarah said while walking quickly toward the house.

While Sarah was getting the cocoa, Emily hooked up the dogs to the sleigh. In a jiffy, Sarah was back with a mug filled to the top with the sweetest smelling hot cocoa and marshmallows.

"Bob oh boy, that sure smells good." Emily smiled as she licked her lips.

"Emily, why are you tying sticks on the dogs' heads?"

"I found the dogs chewing on these sticks and decided it would be a great idea to pretend they are reindeer just like Santa's. The big guy's reindeer have antlers, so ours need them too." She smiled proudly.

They both started sipping the hot sweetness.

With his Southern accent, Fruffy the Saint Bernard barked, "Gollleeeee, Brutus. They took my cotton pickin' stick from me, those ol' thieves. Tell me, tell me, what would it be they took? I'm confused real reeeal bad." He scratched his ear with his paw.

"You old dimwit. What's your bloody problem?" Brutus asked in his English accent.

"Help me, help me, boss. She's a-puttin' it on my big ol' head." Fruffy whined.

"Oh, you big bloke. And exactly what do you call this ridiculous thing on my head, you oversized hairball?"

"*Mmm*, that chocolate drink smells absolutely divine. Can I have a spot of that right here in my mouth?" Brutus asked with his mouth wide open, hoping to catch anything that spilled out of the overly full cup.

"Me too, boss. Can I have some? Can I? Can I? It smells garsh darn good, and I'm sure thirsty." Fruffy barked.

"Fruffy, if you get any closer, she may just swat you with a rolled up classified section of the newspaper just like our last owner. I'm quite sure it would be well deserved. If she in fact truly wanted you to have some, you would have it."

"*Ho ho ho* and Merry Christmas to you, little girl. I'm Santa Claus. And just who might you be?" Emily asked with laughter as she stuck her belly out. She loved to pretend with her little sister.

"My name is Sarah. I am the sweetest, cutest, most adorable little girl you will ever want to meet. Anyone will tell you that. Except don't ask my brother because he thinks girls are totally gross." She laughed.

They laughed hysterically at each other as the sleigh glided smoothly through the untouched snow.

As they rode around to the front of the house, they noticed Mr. Snow's gloomy face.

"Oh no. Mr. Snow looks very sad. Emily, please stop and let's see what's wrong with him."

After Emily stopped the sleigh, they both hopped off and walked over to where Mr. Snow was standing hunched over.

"Mr. Snow, what's the matter?" Emily asked.

"It's all my fault that you're not inside enjoying the party. You and all the other boys and girls are out in this freezing cold weather helping me. I sure wish I would have stayed at the North Pole," he said as a tear trickled down his frosty cheek. "Never before have I met such nice boys and girls like all of you. Santa would be proud to know there are boys and girls like you willing to help an old snowman like me."

"You mean friends, Mr. Snow. We'll be your friends forever and ever," Sarah said gleefully.

They both moved in closer to Mr. Snow and put their arms around him. "We will do whatever it takes to make things right, big guy," Emily said.

"I have a tissue. Let me help wipe away those tears," Sarah said as she gently wiped them away. "So what do you think of our sleigh and reindeer?" she asked.

Mr. Snow hollered, "Wait a minute! Wait a doggone minute! Yippee! Those are my arms. My wonderful, beautiful arms." He bounced up and down.

"We had no idea they were your arms," Emily said, removing them from the dogs' heads. Mr. Snow, why are you crying?" she asked.

"I'm crying happy tears, my dear. I'm happy, happy, happy!"

Emily and Sarah began to slide his arms back into place. Once they were back on, Mr. Snow gave himself the biggest hug.

"Why don't you climb aboard and help us look for the rest of your accessories?" Emily asked.

"Sounds like a snowsational idea, and I do need my accessories, as you call them. I think it would be best for me to stay here and wait for the others to return, but it's sure nice to have my arms back." He smiled. "Now I can use my magical cane for whatever problems may arise."

Mr. Snow walked over to the sleigh and picked up the magical cane. It glittered and lit up as soon as he touched it.

"A special friend gave it to me. Perhaps you know him. A jolly guy in a *ho ho ho* sort of way."

"Santa gave that to you, didn't he?" Sarah asked with excitement.

"Yes, he certainly did," he answered. He held it up, admiring all its magical wonders.

"Maybe Santa will bring me one this year," Emily said.

Mr. Snow knew he owned the only magical cane around. "Perhaps he may someday, little lady."

"Bye, Mr. Snow. We'll see you later," Sarah said.

"Girls, have a wonderful and safe trip."

CHAPTER 9

Several hours later, back at the house, Caroline was adding the finishing touches to the party decorations and delicious food. Most of the guests had arrived, including one of Caroline's best friends, Farmer Newton. He was a kindhearted man who did for others like his father had in his youth. He loved winter, and Christmas was his favorite holiday. He believed the Christmas holiday was reserved for God and children.

Each year he brought his tractor and wagon to the party and gave everyone a ride into the beautiful mountains. He would choose the perfect spot, where he would start a bonfire and roast marshmallows while telling Christmas stories or singing everyone's favorite Christmas songs. Though this year was more difficult for him to get around because of health problems, it didn't keep him from one of his favorite traditions. Caroline was thinking of parties she'd had in the past and how much fun the children had. As she looked out the window at the darkening sky, her concern for the children grew.

"It's getting dark and the children aren't back yet. I hope they are OK," she said.

Farmer Newton struggled to get out of the chair and then slowly with his cane limped over to where Caroline was standing.

"How long have they been gone?" he asked.

"They've been gone for quite some time. I thought they would be back by now."

"Everything will work out. You'll see. I'm really proud of the children for what they're doing. They could be enjoying a fun party, but instead they're helping Mr. Snow," Farmer Newton said.

"I totally agree with you, Farmer Newton," Dean said. Dean was Caroline's son-in-law.

"You're right. I tend to worry far more than I should," she said.

She walked away from the window and back into the kitchen.

Jeremy and Shelby arrived back at the house to find that the others had not returned.

"I wonder if the others are back," Jeremy said.

"I thought we were all going to meet back here," Shelby answered.

"Aw, Mr. Snow is sleeping. Let's not wake him. Let's check and see if Grandma has heard from the others."

"Hello, everyone!" Shelby shouted once they were inside.

Caroline quickly walked over and helped them remove their wet coats and frozen gloves.

"Grandma, have you seen the others?" Jeremy asked curiously.

"No, we haven't seen them yet, but I'm sure they will be back soon." She knelt down beside Jeremy and Shelby. "I'm sure they'll walk through the door at any moment."

"Boy oh boy, the snow is coming down hard," Jeremy said.

"It's snowing lots and lots of soft cotton balls!" Shelby laughed.

"It sure is, sweetie. Tomorrow will be a good day to bring out those old sleighs we have," Dean said.

"Oh yes. Please, daddy. Can we?" Shelby said excitedly.

"We'll see."

As they walked through the kitchen and into the living room, the smell of Christmas filled the air. The scent of freshly baked buttery cookies and homemade bread from hours ago lingered. It was like entering a bakery that had just baked a fresh batch of truly yummy goodies. There was also an aroma from the garland swag that had been carefully hung on the mantel, with beautiful soft velvety bows. Above it was a line of several radiant candles that gave off a scent of cinnamon the kids could almost taste. Right below them was a row of stockings that listed the names of the grandchildren in glittering gold paint.

Beside the warmth and glow of the fireplace stood a spectacular, fragrant pine tree. Each year everyone in the family got together to pick out a tree and decorate it. Some of them traveled many miles to be there for the special occasion. Although it was difficult at times for them to agree upon the exact tree, it had been a tradition for many years and would be for many more to come. On the tree were handmade ornaments from generations gone by. The precious hand-knitted tree skirt wrapped around the bottom of tree as though to keep it warm. It was surrounded by perfectly decorated presents.

The adults sat around the fire, talking and sipping apple cider and coffee and munching on a platter of vegetables and dip that had a slight hint of onion. The children sat very quietly, playing games and snacking on cookies fresh out of the oven. Dean walked over to the fireplace and sat down in an oversized plush fabric chair. It was so old, and a few of the springs were broken, but that didn't keep it from being the most comfortable chair in the house.

"Daddy, I'm so cold." Shelby shivered. She climbed into his lap, put her arms around his neck, and gave him a big kiss on the cheek.

"Thank you, sweetie." He rubbed noses with her and covered her up with a warm velour blanket. She laid her head on his shoulder and started to doze off.

"Dad, we haven't had much time to spend together since you got your new job," Jeremy said.

"I know, and I'm very sorry, but we will all be together on Christmas."

"I can hardly wait." Jeremy smiled.

"Would anyone care for some fresh java?" Caroline asked.

"That would surely warm the iceberg floating around in my stomach," Dean said.

Caroline pulled another batch of cookies out of the oven with one hand and basted Mr. Chubby with the other. Each Christmas Caroline had a contest on who would name the turkey. This year Emily had won the honors of naming the prized bird. It was a twenty-four-pound turkey, and the name Mr. Chubby fit him perfectly.

"Dean, could you please turn on the TV and let's see what's happening with the weather?" Caroline asked.

As he got up to turn on the TV, he moved the lacy curtain and glanced outside. There was a thin glaze of ice on the window, and among all that was so pure stood Mr. Snow, sleeping peacefully.

"*Whew*. The winds are really whipping," Dean said.

"Oh, Dad, we found these for Mr. Snow." Jeremy reached into his jacket and pulled out Mr. Snow's glasses.

"That's wonderful. Why didn't you give them to Mr. Snow?" He looked them over for damage.

"We did not want to wake him." Shelby grinned.

She ran back over, climbed up into his lap again, and covered up with the blanket.

"Well, isn't anyone curious to know where we found them?" Jeremy asked.

"Of course we are," Caroline answered. She sat down on the couch, next to the tree.

"Where might that be?" Dean asked.

"On this cute little baby duck's face. Isn't that the funniest thing you ever heard?" Shelby laughed.

"You've got to be kidding me." Dean laughed.

"How did they get there?" Caroline laughed in disbelief.

"I haven't a clue, but the baby duck wasn't with its mommy, so we rescued it from the pond and took it back over to her," Jeremy said.

Dean knew the response they would give him, but he asked it anyway: "How, young man, did you get across the pond to where the duck was and rescue it?"

"With Grandma's boat," Shelby answered.

Dean jumped up from the couch. "You both could have gotten hurt!"

"What were you two thinking?" Caroline asked.

"Come on, Dad. I took care of Shelby," Jeremy said.

"Oh, please don't be mad at us. We wanted the baby duck to be with its mommy for Christmas." Shelby smiled.

"The baby duck is fine, and so are we, but there was a problem with the boat that we should discuss," Jeremy said. He walked over to them.

"What is it?" Caroline asked.

Jeremy scratched his head, trying to find the right way to tell her.

"Here goes nothing. *Hmm*, let's see. You no longer have a boat. May I have another cookie?"

"It sank, Grandma. If he gets another cookie, I want one too," Shelby said.

"That's OK. It was a very old boat anyway, and now I have an excuse to buy a new one." Caroline smiled. She put her arms around Jeremy and Shelby and handed them both another yummy sugar cookie.

"More importantly, you both are safe," Dean said.

As soon as the meteorologist on TV started to give his forecast, everyone got quiet. They all focused their attention on what he was saying. It was not what they expected.

CHAPTER 10

"COLORADO, BRACE YOURSELVES FOR THE worst storm in history. Record-breaking snowfall, fifty miles per hour winds, drifts, and power outages are expected. Emergency crews will be working around the clock, and the state has requested assistance from all over the country."

Everyone was shocked when they heard this, and all their concern was totally on the children. Caroline put her hand over her mouth as her eyes filled with tears.

She gasped. "I had no idea."

"You wouldn't have known," Dean said.

Farmer Newton slowly got up from the chair he was sitting in and limped over to where they stood. "If you had known, you wouldn't have let the children go out into this horrible weather," he said.

"What is it?" Michelle, Jonathan and Katie's mom, asked as she walked in through the back door. She took her coat off and hung it on the coatrack. "Well, are you going to tell me what's going on or not?"

"Honey, it's like this. Jonathan, Katie, Emily, and Sarah are in the woods, helping a sweet snowman named Mr. Snow find parts that blew away in the fierce wind. He's staying with us for a—" Caroline said.

"And what? What!" she demanded.

"Michelle, what your mom is trying to say is that the national weather channel has issued a storm advisory for tonight. High winds, eight to fifteen inches of fresh snow, and quite possibly avalanches occurring in some areas," Farmer Newton explained.

"It will be getting dark soon, so please tell me they aren't still out in this mess!" Michelle looked around at everyone to get an answer, but the looks on their faces told the truth. "Have you all completely lost your minds?"

"We didn't know about the severe weather conditions until this evening when we watched it on TV," Farmer Newton answered.

"We love them, and there is no way we would have let them go if we knew about the bad weather forecast," Caroline said.

The raised voices woke Mr. Snow up. He peeked curiously through the kitchen window and began to tap on the glass pane. "Hello. Is everything OK?"

Caroline walked over to the door and opened it.

"Why all the long faces?" he asked.

Farm Newton hesitated. "Well, you see, it's like this: there is a terrible storm heading our way that will bring with it a lot more snow and wind."

"Yippee! Sounds like my kind of weather," Mr. Snow cheered.

"Any other time, it would be wonderful to hop on our snowmobiles and ride the big white ones, but the children are still out there," Mr. Newton said.

Mr. Snow's cheering abruptly ended, followed by much concern in his voice. "Oh no, goodness gracious. I must have been sleeping a lot longer than I thought. Let's see. Jeremy and Shelby are here." He looked around.

"Yes, they are, but Emily, Sarah, Katie, and Jonathan aren't," Michelle said.

Shelby walked over to the door, took his hand in hers, and squeezed. "Mr. Snow, they're lost."

"It's all my fault. If anything happens to those dear children, it will be because of me."

Farmer Newton walked over to Mr. Snow, placed his hand on his shoulder, and began to lightly massage away the stress building in him. "Mr. Snow, it's going to be OK," he said.

"No one knew the weather was going to be bad, and they wanted to help you," Dean said.

"I think we should take Farmer Newton's tractor and search for them, but we will need you to help us," Caroline said.

Shelby looked up at Mr. Snow with her pitiful eyes. "Mr. Snow, please. We can't do it without you," she said.

Everyone waited to see what his response would be. He looked down at Shelby and then at everyone else in the room. Mr. Snow looked down again at Shelby's face.

"How could anyone say no to you?" he reached down and squeezed her cheek.

"I don't know about all of you, but I'm going to look for the children," Farmer Newton said. He headed for the door and quickly turned around to study everyone's face.

"I'm right behind you," Dean said. He headed for the coatrack, grabbed his coat, gloves, and hat, and then put them on.

"We're all right behind you," Caroline said.

"Yes, it will be a lot easier with a group of people," Michelle said.

"Come on, ladies. Let's get cracking. We'll meet you guys outside," Caroline instructed.

They quickly gathered up food, blankets, lanterns, flashlights, and anything else they could possibly need. They were moving so quickly, they were like bulls in a china shop.

"Come on, Mr. Snow," Jeremy said. He reached over and took Mr. Snow's hand. "Let's go, pal."

Mr. Snow did not hesitate to go with the others and search for the children. After all, they needed him more than they realized. Little did they know that the precious cane he held in his hand was magical, and it would help save the children.

The men hooked up the tractor to the trailer as Jeremy swept the snow off rickety trailer's seats. "There now we have a place to sit," he said proudly.

"Quick thinking, Jeremy," Dean said.

When it was finally ready, they all squeezed onto the trailer. Mr. Snow took some of the blankets and carefully covered up the children so they would be warm. Then he climbed aboard and sat up front by Farmer Newton. Farmer Newton started up the rusty sounding tractor, and smoke roared from the frozen exhaust pipe.

"Off we go, and where we stop, only I will know." Farmer Newton smiled, though he was really struggling to get the worrisome thoughts out of his mind.

Shelby started singing in her sweet voice. "Farmer Newton had a tractor, *e-i-e-i-o*. And on his tractor sat sweet little me, *e-i-e-i-o*." Everyone chuckled.

CHAPTER 11

"JONATHAN, I'M SO COLD. I can't walk anymore," Katie moaned. Her teeth were chattering, and her nose was running from the cold temperatures.

"OK. Hop on my back, and I will carry you," he said. He stooped down and helped her onto his back. "I can't understand it, Katie. I've been back in these woods tons of times and have never gotten lost before. It will be getting dark soon, and with the snow coming down and the wind blowing, it will be difficult to see, even with the flashlight. Are you OK, Katie?"

"I'm fine. Where are we going?" She shivered.

Jonathan's mind raced with thoughts of never finding their way back, freezing before they could find shelter, or possibly running into the bear that was prowling in the dark, waiting for the right moment to attack. He always had a way of letting his imagination get the better of him. He was a determined young man and knew he would do whatever to protect his baby sister.

"Please don't cry, Katie. Everything is going to be OK, and you know a scout never goes back on his promises," Jonathan said in an exhausted voice. "If only we could find the cave that my friends and I found. We could duck in there until the snow stops falling and the winds die down. Oh how much fun we used to have. All the ghost stories and weenies we roasted. I don't know about you, Katie, but I'm starved."

He kept talking. "Yum yum. I sure could go for one, two, or maybe

35

even three delicious weenies smothered in ketchup and mustard. Oh yeah. And chili cheese fries dripping with ketchup. Uh-huh. That surely would hit the spot and satisfy that animal that's making all that growling racket in my stomach."

Katie slowly lifted her head off his back. "Yummy. Could you please save me one of your wieners, but hold the yellow gunk and, oh yeah, the stinky smelly things."

"Whatever you say." He laughed. "You know, Katie, there's this old hollowed out tree that all of us scouts carved our initials in. If only we could find it, the cave is not far. If we do find it, I don't know if I could let you in if you don't know the secret code word us scouts made up."

"Please. Oh please, Jonathan. I just gotta get in," she begged.

There was a long moment of silence. The only sound they could hear was the breaths Jonathan struggled to take as he slowly moved over the small hills that lay under deep snow. The snow was beginning to mix with sleet, pounding the trees, which were already beginning to freeze over.

"Boy oh boy, Katie, the snow is getting deeper and deeper."

"Hurry, Jonathan. I'm getting colder and colder, and my toes are frozen."

As Jonathan and Katie continued to move through the snow, the wind blew it into drifts. It made it more difficult for them to find the tree they were looking for.

"Oh, I can't go any farther. I need to rest. Katie, please hop off my back." He sat her down by a tree and leaned up against it.

"You OK, Jonathan?"

"I'll be fine."

"I'm sorry you don't feel good."

"It'll be all right. I just need to catch my breath. You must weigh a ton, Katie. What's Mom been feeding you?"

"Lots of peanut butter and jelly sandwiches. It may be the yummy ice cream from last night."

"Good grief. I'm sorry I asked." He chuckled.

"Oh, that's OK, but after I ate it, my big belly hurt so much."

"Mom did tell you not to eat but one bowl, Katie. Maybe next time you'll listen to her."

36

Bang went this loud sound.

"What's that?" She shook with fright.

He stood up and brushed the snow off his legs. "It was a gunshot. Sounds like Uncle Kevin saw a deer."

Suddenly, birds came flying out of the tree they were standing by. "Oh wow. Where did they come from, Jonathan?"

"I guess the gunshot spooked 'em. They must have been staying inside to keep dry. Good grief, Katie. This is the tree we were looking for. It was the one I was leaning against. If it were a snake, it would have bit us."

"Are there snakes in the snow, Jonathan?"

Jonathan just shrugged and laughed.

They slowly crept up to the cave and peered in. Jonathan hesitated, knowing the possible dangers that lurked inside its deep, dark tunnels.

CHAPTER 12

AS THEY SLOWLY WALKED THROUGH the entrance, there was a tunnel to the right and one to the left.

"OK, sis. We have to make a decision," Jonathan said.

"I always do 'eeny meeny miny mo' to help me. What do you think?"

"Well, Katie, I … oh, OK. Why don't you do it?"

"OK. Eeny meeny miny mo. My mom told me to pick you." She pointed to the left tunnel.

"Left it is," Jonathan said. He pointed the flashlight toward the left tunnel and took Katie's hand.

"I'm so scared, Jonathan. What if the bear's here?" She wrapped her arms around his waist and held on tightly.

"Katie, please. I can hardly move. Everything is going to be OK. I promise," he said.

She loosened her grip.

"Please stay calm, Katie. Nothing is going to happen. Wouldn't you rather be here than out in the freezing cold snow?" he asked.

As they made their way through the twisting and turning tunnel, they noticed a flicker of light in the distance. Jonathan hesitated, not knowing who could possibly be in there with them. Could it be someone evil, possibly a hunter resting, or maybe simply a man or woman who was stranded or lost?

"Uh-oh. Someone left the light on. Mommy tells us never to leave the light on and waste electricity," Katie reminded him.

"Just stay behind me. I don't know who's in there with us." He grabbed her arm and pushed her behind him.

"I'm so scared," she whimpered.

"No big deal. Someone just had the same idea we had to find shelter until the storm blew over."

As they slowly and cautiously rounded the corner, they were surprised to see the ones in the cave were not evil after all. They were both relieved when they saw Emily and Sarah. Jonathan ran over and embraced Sarah and gave Emily a high five.

"Are you guys OK?" he asked.

"We're fine. We just got lost and were lucky to find your old scout cave and get in out of the cold," Emily replied.

"I'm so glad you are not out in the snow. Have you seen Jeremy and Shelby?"

"Nope, we haven't." Sarah said.

"Hey, how did you girls manage to make a fire?" he asked.

"I had a couple of matches with me and started it. We're always prepared." Emily smiled.

"Yep, that's my motto." Jonathan laughed. He gave Sarah and Emily each a high five.

"Oh, you're in big trouble playing with matches. Mommy never lets me play with matches," Katie said.

"Me either." Sarah shook her head.

"That's because you aren't a scout like me. That fire sure does feel good," he said. Jonathan squatted down and pulled his gloves off his very cold hands and held them up near the fire. He was thinking how funny it was that such a small fire put out so much heat. "It feels sooooo good. Come on, Katie. Warm your hands," he said.

He helped her remove her gloves and hat, which was soaked from all the falling snow and sleet.

"Sarah and I found some wood. And some berries to eat too. Are you guys hungry?" Emily asked.

"Sure thing. We both are starved," Jonathan replied.

"I only ate two. I thought they were nasty." Sarah chuckled. She stuck her tongue out and quickly spit as if trying to remove the disgusting taste from her mouth.

"Come on, Katie. They're pretty darn good," Jonathan said.

"No way, José. They probably taste yucky like liver. Blah and more blah."

"Oh, your mommy makes you eat liver too?" Sarah asked.

"Yep, she sure does. She says it's good for red blood. Whatever that's supposed to mean."

Jonathan chucked at the in-depth conversation they were having over something as trivial as liver. When all he could think about was getting home before freezing. But he figured that if their minds were on food, they wouldn't be worried about being stranded and lost in a dark cold cave.

"The fire is warm but not warm enough to keep us from freezing," Jonathan said. He picked up a small stick and started moving around the piece of wood that had not burned.

"You're right. The only way to stay warm enough is to make sure the fire doesn't go out, and if we huddle together, that will help," Emily said.

The girls moved in closer to one another. Jonathan plopped down by the fire and leaned up against the side of the cave.

"Boy oh boy, I'm pooped. Come on, girls. Let's try to get some shuteye. Some rest will do us a world of good," he said.

Before long, all the girls had fallen fast asleep. Everyone except for Jonathan. He couldn't stop worrying about the others. He knew the only way for them to make it back safely was for him to go for help. He quickly and quietly gathered his backpack, put his hat and gloves back on, threw a couple pieces of wood onto the warm fire, gave each of the girls a kiss on the forehead, and headed toward the entrance.

"I'm the oldest, and it's my responsibility to look out for the others. God, please watch over them and keep them safe in your arms while I'm gone," he prayed to himself. He felt comfort knowing God would watch over them and that they had a warm fire and berries should they get hungry. There was always snow they could eat if they got thirsty.

CHAPTER 13

THE NIGHT WAS BEGINNING TO settle in, and everyone was beginning to get tired from the long ride. Some of the children were even sleeping. Farmer Newton was heading in the direction Jeremy told him to go, and they were not far from the cave.

"Farmer Newton, we've come a long way. Once we find the children, I don't think they will be up to making the trip back. I just pray that Jeremy is right about them being in the cave," Caroline said.

"Why don't we stay in the barn and let the children get some rest?" Farmer Newton suggested.

"Well, we do have plenty of food and blankets to keep us warm. I don't know about you, but I'm exhausted." Caroline yawned.

Jeremy peeped out of one eye. "Sounds like a winner to me," he said.

"Oh, Daddy. An adventure." Shelby clapped.

"How can anyone talk about sleep when the children are out there stranded? God only knows where," Michelle demanded.

"Michelle, with everything considered, that is the best option," Farmer Newton said.

"Honey, he's right. If we don't get some rest, we won't have the strength to continue looking," Caroline said.

"You better hope they're in the cave or I'm looking for them myself. I don't care how dark or cold it is or tired I get. I will not give up until we find them," Michelle said and slammed her fist into the side of the trailer.

"Aunt Michelle, I know Jonathan is in the cave. He's way too smart to not go into it for shelter," Jeremy said.

"I hope you're right. I surely hope you're right."

It was hard to believe that the weather could get any worse than it already was. But all at once, the soft powdery snow that was falling turned to ice. The ice balls were tremendous in size, the biggest they had ever seen.

"Ouch, Daddy. Someone's shooting at us," Shelby said. She tucked her head under Dean's arm to shield her face from the stinging sleet.

"Honey, it's not gunshots. It's very, very large ice," Dean said.

Everyone grabbed blankets to protect the children and themselves from the pounding sleet. As Farmer Newton peeked out from under the blanket, he noticed everything was covered in ice. The trees looked like a donut covered in a glaze. He was concerned when he noticed the tops of the trees leaning over from the weight of it.

"Mr. Snow, look at all the ice on the trees," Farmer Newton said nervously.

"Jeremy, hold the blanket over you and your sister's heads so I can talk to Mr. Snow and Farmer Newton," Dean said. "Hey, guys. Are you thinking the same thing I am?"

"The weight of this heavy snow and ice is not good for these trees. They are going to start snapping off and crashing down to the ground," Farmer Newton said.

"That's exactly what I was thinking, but we can't turn back now," Dean said. "We just need to be extra cautious and keep an eye out for any falling trees," he exclaimed.

Almost instantly after he said it, there was an incredibly loud snap. They looked around to see which tree was on the way to the ground.

"It's that one!" Caroline screamed, pointing at an enormous dead oak in front of the tractor that was coming down. On its way to the ground, it was taking many small trees down with it.

Everyone stood up in complete terror as they witnessed the trees fall right in front of their eyes. Shelby trembled, closed her eyes tightly, and held her daddy's hand with all her might. Their screams were so loud, they could be heard throughout the hills.

When the oak hit the ground, it shook with tremendous force. It felt like an earthquake was rocking the ground beneath them. It was quite possibly the loudest sound they had ever heard.

"Oh my gosh, Dad. It almost hit us!" Jeremy shouted.

Dean hesitated. "I know, but we're OK." He flopped back down and breathed a huge sigh of relief. Nothing else was said for at least a minute or two. Most of their thoughts were focused on how close the tree had come to falling on them.

"Daddy, is it over?" Shelby cried.

"Yes, honey, it is. You can open your eyes."

"Wow, what a huge tree," Jeremy said.

"I don't suppose anyone needs any firewood. Do ya?" Mr. Snow said with giddy charm.

"I don't know about any of you, but that little incident surely worked me up into a sweat. *Whew*. I've warmed up," Caroline said.

"If that's the only way to get warm, forget it." Jeremy chuckled.

"Huh. Well, what are you going to do about this obstacle, Mr. Snow?" Michelle asked.

Everyone looked at him, waiting for a response.

"That tree is too large for us to go around, and the woods are too crowded with trees for us to get through," Farmer Newton said.

Mr. Snow got a gleam in his eye, grabbed his cane, and bounded off the trailer. "Everyone please stay put, and I will take care of this tree situation," he said confidently. With a big burst of energy, he slid over to the tree. "Thank you, Santa, for this most helpful gift," he whispered under his breath as he looked up into the sky.

Everyone watched with complete curiosity, wondering how he would eliminate the problem at hand.

He stretched out both arms and slid his hands underneath the tree. "Heave ho," he said and began to lift the tree effortlessly like picking up a feather. He then turned it around so it was out of the way and dropped it. *Bam* went the tree again.

Everyone cheered and clapped their hands.

"Yeah, Mr. Snow!"

"Way to go, Mr. Snow," Caroline cheered.

"You're a cool dude." Jeremy laughed.

"I'm bad, oh yeah. I'm a cool dude right down to the snow bone," Mr. Snow said in a childlike manner.

Everyone sat back down. Dean covered up the children again, and within minutes they were on their way.

"Boy oh boy, what a night this has been," Dean said.

"If it weren't for you, Mr. Snow, we never would have made it through. You sure are a very special snowman with many talents," Caroline said.

"Oh there's plenty I can't do, but I appreciate the compliment anyhow." He smiled and placed his arm around Farmer Newton's shoulder. "Now let's find those children!" Mr. Snow shouted.

CHAPTER 14

JEREMY WAS THE ONLY CHILD that didn't fall asleep from exhaustion. Even with all the ice coming down and the bitter cold temperatures, Farmer Newton and Mr. Snow settled back down to endure the struggle it took for the tractor to get through the deep snow. They dodged all the trees that had fallen from the heavy snow and ice that had settled on them. Even over the roaring sound of the tractor going up and over the hills, they could still hear the echoes of trees falling.

The path they were taking was the same one they took year after year. It was then that Farmer Newton realized the path they were taking wasn't a good one. He had completely forgotten about the canyon with the snow ledge that suspended out over where they were traveling. He thought about the amount of snow that had fallen and the how the forecaster had called for possible avalanches. If there were an avalanche, this would be the spot for one.

"Farmer Newton, you're mighty quiet. Is everything OK?" Mr. Snow asked.

Farmer Newton stopped the tractor, and the jolt it made woke up those who were sleeping. "I'm not sure if I want to take a chance on going through the canyon with the tractor."

"We've done it every year. Why would there be a problem now?" Caroline asked.

Farmer Newton turned off the tractor so everyone could hear him better and then turned around to look at them all. He hesitated. "Well

47

it's like this. All the heavy snow and ice lying on the ledge is not a good thing."

"What do you mean?" Michelle asked.

Farmer Newton continued, "I'm afraid it can't take the loud sounds of the tractor, and I'm not sure if I want to risk a possible avalanche."

"If we don't go through the canyon, we will have to go back the way we came," Dean said.

"That's crazy. We will never make it to the cave in time," Michelle said.

"Nobody asked me, but I say we take a chance with the tractor," Jeremy said.

"Me too. It's our only hope to rescue the children," Caroline said.

"Let's see a show of hands. All those wanting to turn back, raise your hands. Just as I suspected. Not a single hand. OK, onward we go," Farmer Newton said.

He turned back around and fired up the tractor. They were off again, hoping they would make it through the canyon without being trapped in an avalanche. Dean held on tightly to Shelby and Jeremy. Tension was high in the bitter cold air as they gripped the sides of the wagon.

As the tractor roared like a freight train, they began to slowly move through the canyon. It was a miracle how the old tractor was still running after what it had gone through. Just when they were almost out of possible danger, there was an enormous roar. It sounded like a jet plane taking off. They could hear the snow starting to fall down the steep mountainside, shaking the trailer they were still sitting in.

"Avalanche!" Farmer Newton yelled. He jumped off the tractor and took off running as quickly as he could.

"Run and get out of the way of the snow!" Mr. Snow shouted.

Grabbing what they could, they frantically bolted off the trailer and took off running right behind Farmer Newton. Mr. Snow grabbed Shelby as he slid behind a huge rock.

Everyone followed Mr. Snow and braced for the snow.

Without giving it a second thought, Jeremy took off running back to the tractor for Mr. Snow's magic cane.

"Jeremy, no!" Mr. Snow yelled.

Jeremy was unable to find it, but he wasn't about to give up. He could only think of how important the cane was to Mr. Snow and not about the serious danger he was in.

"Hurry up and run!" they all shouted.

Mr. Snow slid over to Jeremy, reached into the trailer, and grabbed the cane.

Shelby started bawling. "Mr. Snow, save Jeremy," she yelled.

Immediately Mr. Snow did a belly flop into the snow and Jeremy jumped on his back. "Hold on tight," he said.

Jeremy wrapped one hand around Mr. Snow's neck and tightly gripped the cane with the other. Mr. Snow zipped through the snow just like a bobsled going eighty miles per hour. They all cheered.

"Look at him go!" Shelby laughed.

They couldn't believe how fast Mr. Snow could travel on his belly. He was easily outrunning the snow that was moving in closely behind him. Once they were all safely tucked behind the rock, they braced themselves. Finally, when it was all over, the snow was as high as the rock they were crouched behind. Michelle climbed up onto the mound of snow and started walking.

"This has been a lot of fun, but I'm going to rescue our children," she said.

"Where are you going?" Dean asked.

"What does it look like? I'm walking to the cave," she answered.

"I guess plan B is where we stand now," Dean said.

Michelle bellowed out, "There is no plan B. Have you taken a good look at the deep snow?"

"There is no way we can get through this. It's a good thing we were behind this rock. Otherwise, we'd be buried under God only knows how much snow," Farmer Newton said.

This surprised everyone because they all knew how patient Farmer Newton was. Even Michelle stopped to listen to him.

Mr. Snow placed his hand on Farmer Newton's shoulder. "It's going to be OK. Remember I told you it's all going to be OK. Now, how about we take a moment to call a dear friend of mine. I know he will help get us out of this snowy situation we're in. Jeremy, my boy, will you please hand me my cane?"

"You got it, Mr. Snow." Jeremy smiled.

"What do you suppose he'll pull out of it this time?" Dean asked.

"I'm sure we'll see soon enough." Caroline chuckled.

Mr. Snow pressed a button that had gone unnoticed until that moment. A peculiar musical sound came from the cane as the top extended out into a long pole. It looked like propellers extending from a big helicopter. They watched with curiosity as out popped a black box with some sort of handle on it. The children scooted in closer to get a better look at the strange object.

Could he be trying to contact someone from another planet? Perhaps some planet they weren't aware of? Or maybe Mr. Snow wanted to show off some more of his magical talents? He started talking without even noticing that the others had moved in close enough to touch him. Curiosity was up, and so were their ears as they saw a TV pop from the top of the box.

"Excuse me, please." Mr. Snow smiled. He looked around at all the faces peering at him.

There on the screen was the one and only Santa Claus, with his rosy colored cheeks, white hair everywhere, happy jolly smile, and a chubby belly that shook just like jelly. Wow! He looked just like all the parents had described.

Shelby jumped up and down, clapping her hands. "Ooh, Daddy! It's Santa! It's Santa!" she chanted.

"I see him, but I don't believe it," Michelle said. She rubbed her eyes like she was just waking up. "I'm still asleep and all this must be a dream. Someone please pinch me so I can wake up. Never mind. I'll do it myself." She pinched her own cheek with her fingers, which were covered by thick gloves.

"What's the matter, Aunt Michelle? You don't believe in Santa?" Jeremy asked.

"Well, I ah …"

"Just as we've long suspected." Jeremy laughed.

"I've believed in you my whole life, and my daddy believes in you too. Don't you, Daddy?"

"Why of course I do, sweetie," Dean said. He looked over at Michelle with a slight smile.

"Hi, Santa." Mr. Snow smiled.

"Well, if it isn't my best friend, Mr. Snow. I've been waiting for your call. I hope you're getting all that well-needed rest."

"I am, Santa, but—"

"Children, *shhh*," Caroline interrupted.

With all the children hollering to Santa their wish lists, Mr. Snow was having a hard time hearing him.

"*Ho ho ho* and Merry Christmas, boys and girls," Santa said.

"Santa, I've been a real good girl. Right, Daddy?" Shelby said. "Do you remember my name?"

"How could I possibly forget your name?" Santa smiled.

"I'm the one with two sissies and one brother. Three to be exact, and we live in the house with the red door and fuzzy kitty."

"You've been a very good girl this year."

"Do you know what I want for Christmas?"

"Shelby, Santa knows what you want for Christmas, but please let him talk to Mr. Snow." Dean chuckled.

All the adults gathered the children up and moved them away from Mr. Snow so he could talk to Santa without any more interruptions.

"Santa, I'm in a slight bind."

"Say no more, Mr. Snow. I know what's going on. What I'll do is send you three of my best elves with my backup sleigh to you and the others. For now I've got to go. Remember, it's Christmas Eve and I have a lot to do. Bye, Mr. Snow."

"See you soon, Santa," Mr. Snow answered.

"*Ho ho ho*. Bye-bye, boys and girls. And Merry Christmas," Santa said gleefully.

CHAPTER 15

SANTA PICKED UP HIS GLITTERING red-and-w
cane phone and called the toy factory.

"Toy factory, head elf in charge Clarissa speaking. H
help you?"

"Clarissa, it's me, Santa."

"Oh hi, Santa. How may I help you?"

"Could you, Tiffany, and Wanda come in here for a minu
has a special project for you."

"Sure thing, Santa. We'll be glad to help," Clarissa sang.

Santa hung up the phone, leaned back in his chair, picke
Christmas list, and continued working. "*Hmm*, let me see. Li
was a good boy this year, but little Cindy was quite bad," San
softly to himself.

Instantly there was a knock on his door. "Santa, it's us,"
said. She slowly pushed the door open to Santa's Christmas offi

"Hi, girls. Come on over here and sit down beside Santa. I
talk to you."

The elves were short and very chubby, just like Santa, and all
up in green and curly shoes with bells on the tips. Clarissa had v
for Santa for 50 years and had recently been promoted to head elf,
known as manager in charge.

Wanda was second in charge under Clarissa and had been nickr
"workaholic" by the rest of the elves. She was much chubbier
most of the others. Not only did she work in the toy factory, bu

so worked in Santa's Delights—a shop run by Mrs. Claus. It made the most scrumptious goodies you could eat. It was built only 30 years ago for children who asked Santa for candy at Christmas. Wanda knew Clarissa would be retiring soon, so she wanted to be ready to fill the role of manager in charge. She was Clarissa's shadow, so she did everything Clarissa did and everything she said. She got on Clarissa's nerves sometimes, but Santa reminded Clarissa that Wanda loved her so much that she wanted to be just like her.

Tiffany was the bashful one, with big blue eyes and curly eyelashes. The elves referred to her as Grace. Well, because she fell a lot.

Tiffany walked over to Santa, carrying a beautifully wrapped package with his name written in big bold letters. "Santa, I made this for you." She smiled while batting her eyelashes. As she handed Santa the gift, she stumbled over the corner of his chair, and gift flew up in the air. It landed right in his arms. "Oops. Sorry about that, Santa." She smiled.

"We should change your name to Fumble Fingers." Clarissa laughed.

"We should change your name to Fumble Fingers." Wanda laughed.

"Why thank you, big blue eyes. That's very sweet of you to remember Santa at Christmas."

Tiffany began to rock back and forth nervously while kicking her cute little pointed feet around. "Shucks. You're welcome, Santa," she said bashfully.

"You have a project for us, Santa?" Clarissa asked.

"You have a project for us, Santa?" Wanda also asked.

"I sure do, girls. It seems as though our good friend Mr. Snow has gotten himself into a jam."

"As in peanut butter and jam?" Tiffany quietly asked.

Santa laughed. Every time he turned around, the elves said something that tickled him into laughing. "You three are just too much. How about if I tell you all about the little job I need you to do for me?" Then Santa explained to them what he needed them to do.

CHAPTER 16

ALL THE OTHERS WERE WAITING for Mr. Snow to pull some more magic out of his cane. Mr. Snow noticed everyone looking at him with worrisome expressions on their faces.

"Please quit worrying. Didn't I tell you that I had another one of my snowsational ideas? Help is on the way. Just try to stay warm."

By now, some of the adults were not as worried as they had been. They knew Mr. Snow wouldn't let them down. They turned their flashlights off to conserve the batteries and sat there quietly in the dark, listening to the wind howling and feeling the snow falling on their cold faces. The children's thoughts drifted back to seeing Santa. Their sweet Christmassy dreams slipped into a fairyland of their own, filled with lots and lots of wishes on what Santa would bring them on Christmas Eve to tear into on exciting Christmas Day. How much fun daydreaming, or even night dreaming, could be with the different lands they could visit in their minds, just like in a fairy-tale book filled with so many delightful things.

Meanwhile, the elves were on their way to the rescue.

"Clarissa, do you know where we're going?" Tiffany asked.

"Of course I do!" Clarissa exclaimed.

"Of course I do!" Wanda exclaimed. "Anyhow, the deer are leading the way." She smiled.

"OK, but does Santa know you failed your test at sleigh riding school? That makes it seven times in a row that you failed it." Tiffany smiled.

57

"Why do you stress so much over something as minor as a license?" Clarissa moaned.

"Why do you stress so much over something as minor as a license?" Wanda moaned.

"I don't know," Tiffany said.

"Wanda, do not repeat this. Gee whiz. All you A types need to take a break from worrying. All it does is give you gray elf hair before your time. You know not all the elves have their licenses. Do they?" Clarissa asked.

"Well, no. But … what is an A type?" Tiffany hesitated.

"*Phfff.* Hello? Someone that's hyper beyond describing. Anyway, I'm the one Santa put in charge, so give me a break. There is another matter I would like to quickly bring up. Wanda, I've known for some time that you want my job when I retire soon, but please stop repeating everything I say. It's annoying me. At least for an hour or two."

"Whatever you say, manager in charge." Wanda turned and patted Tiffany on the shoulder. "You and I know who the A type is on this ride. Don't we?" She flopped her round body onto the back seat of the sleigh. "Boy of boy, I'm pooper dooed." She yawned.

"You've been keeping a busy schedule, and Santa said you need to rest," Clarissa said.

"Yeah, I know, but I love working for Mrs. Claus and all the yummies. *Mmm.* I get hungry just thinking about it," Wanda said.

"I understand that, but I overheard Mrs. Claus telling Santa you were eating more than you were producing."

"What can I say? I'm a growing elf, and I need my nutrition." She chuckled.

"Nutrition is one thing, but twenty pounds of chocolate a day? Can you slow it down just a tad? Mrs. Claus can't keep letting your suit out," Clarissa explained.

"Clarissa is right. Your buttons are ready to pop open." Tiffany smiled.

"Santa understands me. He smiles at me all the time."

"He smiles because he doesn't know how you can eat so much candy." Clarissa laughed.

Tiffany laughed too.

"Grace, why don't you sit with Clarissa, and I can get some sleepy peepy and dream of visions of chocolate candy drops dancing in my head?" Wanda instructed.

"OK, workaholic. Uh-oh! Oh no!" Tiffany yelled. As she was moving from one seat to the other, she tripped. Suddenly she was hanging, suspended upside down in midair, with one foot hooked around the blade of the sleigh. Then in a calm and collected voice, she muttered one simple word: "Help. Could I get some help here?"

Wanda and Clarissa peeked out over the edge of the sleigh and noticed Tiffany dangling and swinging by one foot.

"Grace, are you OK?" Wanda asked.

"Silly me. I tripped." Tiffany smiled.

"Go figure. Who would have thought?" Clarissa laughed.

CHAPTER 17

"MR. SNOW, I'M GETTING COLD. Who's coming to rescue us?" Jeremy said.

"Help is on the way." Mr. Snow smiled.

Jingle, jingle went the bells on the sleigh as the elves made a perfectly smooth landing in an open field not far away, which was a surprise, considering who was sitting behind the sleigh wheel.

"Perfect landing as usual," Clarissa announced as she stood up proudly.

Tiffany stood up and gently shook Wanda, who was sleeping soundly. "Workaholic, wake up. We're here," she said.

"Not now. Leave me alone. I was having such a delicious dream." Wanda smiled.

"We have to help Mr. Snow out of … What did Santa call it?" Tiffany asked.

"I think it was a jam," Wanda bellowed.

"Mr. Snow is the sweetest snowman, but he sure has a way of getting into mischief." Clarissa laughed.

"He's surely lucky to have us in sticky situations," Tiffany said.

Wanda rubbed the sand monsters out of her eyes, stretched, and then stretched some more before getting off the sleigh.

"Are you coming, workaholic?" Clarissa asked.

Before Clarissa hopped off the sleigh, she grabbed the Mr. Snow finder that Santa had given her. It was a square device that looked a lot like the ones people used at fancy restaurants when their tables were ready. The Mr. Snow finder sent signals, letting Clarissa know which direction Mr. Snow was in. With the lights on the sleigh, it was as bright as day.

Clarissa turned around and hollered, "Come on, girls. The beep is coming from that direction." She pointed toward the woods.

Clarissa walked up beside Farmer Newton as she shined the light on her chubby face. "Hi there." She smiled as she waved at him.

"It's an alien," Shelby shouted.

"Wait a minute. It's not aliens. These are my good friends Clarissa, Wanda, and Tiffany. They are Santa's little helpers, and they're here to rescue us from the avalanche," Mr. Snow announced.

"Of course. We knew it all along." Caroline snickered.

Shelby walked over to Tiffany and checked her out from head to toe with her flashlight for about five minutes.

"Oh, Daddy, isn't she so cute?" Shelby asked.

Dean laughed. "She sure is."

Quickly Tiffany scooted behind Clarissa and peeped out around her.

"She's a little shy." Clarissa smiled.

"She's a little shy." Wanda smiled.

Shelby walked over to Tiffany and took her hand in hers.

"It's OK, Tiffany. We won't hurt you. Santa knows I'm a real good girl, and I bet you're a real good elf. We can be best buddies. OK?"

"OK." Tiffany batted her lashes bashfully.

After all the introductions were made, everyone quickly loaded onto the sleigh, and it smoothly went up, up, up into the sky like a roller coaster before making the deep plunge down a steep hill to everyone's excitement. They were soon flying above all the clouds. There was no snow, and the moon was so full. If they looked hard enough, they might have been able to see the man in the moon. For a while, no one knew what to say.

"Daddy, Daddy, look how small everything looks from way up here," Shelby said as she looked over the side of the sleigh.

"You're right, Shelby. It sure does."

"Grandma, I think I just saw your house." Jeremy smiled.

Caroline leaned over the side of the sleigh very cautiously and looked down. "I think you're right. *Woo wee.* Don't look down. It's a lulu," she said.

"Come now. You're not scared of heights, are you?" Mr. Snow asked.

"Maybe just a little bit."

Their laughter could be heard for miles and miles. Santa's reindeer knew exactly where to go, as if they had been given special instructions by the big guy himself.

"May I have your attention? This is your elf captain in charge speaking. Please put your seats in their upright positions. Keep all hands and feet inside the sleigh. We are about to land at Paradise Cave. Thank you for flying with us," Clarissa announced.

"May I have your attention? This is your elf captain in charge speaking. Please put your seats in their upright positions. Keep all hands and feet inside the sleigh. We are about to land at Paradise Cave, and thank you for flying with us," Wanda also announced.

"Mr. Snow, why does Wanda say everything Clarissa does?" Jeremy asked.

"My boy, she's been doing that ever since she found out Clarissa will be retiring soon. She's hoping to fill those curlicue shoes of hers." Mr. Snow grinned.

"Oh yeah, I can understand that." Jeremy laughed.

The sleigh glided through the snow as they came to a smooth stop.

CHAPTER 18

THE MEN WERE THE FIRST to leap off the sleigh and head toward the cave. They noticed the snow was covering the entrance.

"Oh no. The avalanche must have hit here too," Dean said.

"Blast it all. Blast it all. What other obstacles will we have to face before we can save the children?" Michelle yelled. She fell to the ground and sobbed. She sat with snow up to her waist, unfazed by the powdery substance.

This was too much for Mr. Snow to bear. He didn't know how to comfort a mother who yearned to have her children safe in her arms.

Caroline wrapped her arms around her, pulling her to her feet. "Michelle, you can't give up. We need you to be strong for the children. They need their mother."

"There's no time to waste. Let's get to digging," Dean hollered.

"With what?" Farmer Newton asked.

"That's right. The shovels were lost in the avalanche," Caroline said.

Everyone turned and looked at Mr. Snow. Mr. Snow scratched his head as he thought about what could be done. "I've got it. Why didn't I think of this sooner? I'll use my handy-dandy propellers to drive us through that snow. Stand back and let me do my snow duty." He smiled.

"Please do." Dean grinned and moved away from the front of the cave.

Clarissa, Wanda, and Tiffany squatted down in the snow and covered their heads with their arms to shield themselves.

"Look out! He's gonna get ya!" Clarissa yelled.

"Look out! He's gonna get ya!" Wanda yelled.

"What are you talking about?" Caroline asked.

"You'll see." Tiffany smiled.

Suddenly, Mr. Snow's arms started spinning in a circular motion. They went faster and faster until they couldn't speed up more. Snow flew everywhere. The humans couldn't believe their eyes as they watched him plow through the snow with his handy-dandy propellers just like a tractor with a plow.

Mr. Snow was having so much fun, he was singing a quaint little tune: "I've been working on the cave, oh, plowing the time away. I've been working on the cave, oh, just to spin my arms all the way ..."

"Look at him go." Clarissa laughed.

"Look at him go." Wanda laughed.

"You go, snowman. Talk about a snowball fight. I want you on my team. You're the snow bomb, Mr. Snow," Jeremy cheered.

Everyone was covering their faces and heads from the snow, but it didn't help. Before they knew it, he had broken through to the entrance of the cave. He was really tired but felt wonderful knowing the children would finally be saved.

Michelle was the first to fly by Mr. Snow and into the cave. The others were close behind her, with Mr. Snow, Farmer Newton, and the elves bringing up the rear. Michelle screamed the children's names as they frantically searched. The deeper they slipped into the cave, the colder it was.

"There's no way the children could survive in here," Farmer Newton whispered under his breath.

Mr. Snow put his finger up to his mouth. "*Shh*. Everyone be quiet and listen. If everyone is shouting, we may not hear them."

"Mr. Snow's right. Everyone please be quiet," Caroline said.

Everyone stopped talking, and in the distance, they heard a faint sound. Was it one of the children calling out? Or was it something or someone else lurking in the mysterious cave?

"It's Katie. It's Katie. I know it," Michelle shouted, her voice echoing through the cave. "Katie, it's Mommy! Where are you?"

"We're here," the voice called back.

"Be quiet, everybody. We don't want to cause all the snow in and around the cave to come down again. We would be in a bad situation," Farmer Newton said.

"Men, come with me," Mr. Snow said.

The women and children watched as the men slipped deeper into the cave.

Within minutes, they heard voices getting louder. Had they found the children, or were they coming back because they couldn't go any farther? As they watched with anticipation, around the corner came Mr. Snow carrying Katie. She was wrapped up in a coat, and her head was lying quietly on Mr. Snow's shoulder. Even though she looked exhausted, she was going to be OK. Following right behind Mr. Snow was Dean carrying Emily and Farmer Newton struggling to carry Sarah with one hand and his cane in the other. But where was Jonathan? He was the only one they didn't see.

Michelle ran over and scooped Katie up as happy tears rolled down her face. "Oh, my sweet baby. Where's Jonathan?" she asked.

Caroline wrapped both arms around Sarah and Emily.

"He went for help. When we heard the voices, we thought he was with you," Sarah said.

"No. He's not with us," Michelle said.

"Jeremy told us about this cave, and we took a chance that you would be here. That's how we knew," Caroline said.

"There's an old barn nearby. How about if we take the children there so they can rest a little before we start back to the house?" Farmer Newton said.

"Are we just going to forget about Jonathan?" Michelle yelled.

"Michelle, right now you need to focus on getting Katie warm. Once the winds die down a little, the men and I can look for Jonathan," Mr. Snow said.

"Sounds like the best thing to do," Caroline said.

Katie pulled on her mother's coat to get her attention. "Mommy, who are they?" she asked as she pointed toward the elves.

Clarissa walked over to Katie and bowed. "We're Santa's elves. At your service, miss," she said, reaching up and patting her on the head.

"This is Clarissa, Wanda, and where did Tiffany go?" Mr. Snow said. He looked around but couldn't find the third bashful elf, who peeked out from behind Emily.

"Mommy, she's a cutie." Katie laughed.

"Yes, she is a cute little rascal."

"Can I please take her home with me to play house?" Katie asked.

"Honey, you act like she's a dog or a cat."

"She's right, Katie. Tiffany plays a big important part in getting the toys ready for Christmas every year. I'm sure Santa couldn't do it without her." Mr. Snow smiled.

"Oh, OK," Katie said, disappointed.

The excitement was indescribable when the children found out they would be taking a fun-filled ride on the best thing around: Santa Claus's spare sleigh.

"Hey, Mr. Snow. We can't all fit on the sleigh. Could you, would you, please make it bigger so we can all fit?" Tiffany blushed.

"Only for you, big blue eyes."

With the help of his cane, Mr. Snow fixed it so it would be a comfortable ride for everyone.

CHAPTER 19

THEY LANDED IN FRONT OF the barn in what seemed like seconds. Off they bounded and headed toward the building that would shelter them from the storm.

"Mommy, I'm hungry," Katie said.

"I know, sweetie. We all are."

"We all are starving," Jeremy said. He patted his growling stomach.

"I guess with all the distractions, we haven't given much thought to eating," Caroline said.

"We didn't have time to get the food or sleeping bags off the trailer," Jeremy said.

"We sure didn't, but the barn will keep us warm and dry," Farmer Newton said.

Many of them turned on their flashlights to get a good look at where they would be staying and hopefully getting a little sleep. The full moon shone over the worn and decrepit old barn, playing peekaboo with the clouds. They could hear the ice pelting the old roof that had once been red but was now covered with rust. There were two windows at the top of the barn on either side. The shutters that had once kept the cold air and animals out were now rotten. The wind was knocking them up against the sides of the barn.

As they entered through the old, heavy door, they noticed some movement behind a big pile of hay.

"Daddy, Daddy, I'm scared," Emily said.

"Hello. Anyone there?" Mr. Snow asked.

"It could be an animal, Daddy," Emily said.

"Quite possibly the most ferocious lion." Jeremy growled.

"Stop it, Jeremy. You're scaring your sister!" Dean said.

"I'm sorry. Just trying to have a little fun." Jeremy grinned.

Everyone shined their flashlights all around the barn.

"I'm going to see what it is," Mr. Snow said. He slid over to a large pile of hay and shined his light all around it to see what was making the noise.

"I don't see anything. Our ears must be playing tricks on us."

"Achoo!"

"OK. Does nothing sneeze, Mr. Snow?" Jeremy asked.

"I've never heard any animals sneeze like that," Sarah said.

"Achoo!"

They all huddled in a group and slowly moved toward the pile of hay.

"Achoo!"

"Here we go again," Jeremy said.

"Someone sure has a bad cold." Emily giggled.

They slowly inched their way closer, keeping their lights shining.

Mr. Snow abruptly stopped and gasped. "Oh my," he said.

"What is it, Mr. Snow?" Jeremy asked.

Jeremy shined his light in the same direction as Mr. Snow's, and when he did, everyone was able to see what was making all the noise. Standing in front of them was a woman and her two children. The little girl's short hair was chopped off in an uneven fashion. Beside her was a young boy who was probably her brother. He wore a tattered baseball hat, boots that had no laces, and a pair of muddy pants. The mother's coat had rips in it, and she wore dirty sweatpants. All of them wore hats, scarves, and gloves with holes in them.

They looked like a very hungry mouse had been nibbling on them.

Emily tugged on Mr. Snow's arm. "Who are they?" she asked.

"I don't know," he replied.

It was clear to the adults that they were homeless, but who were they and how long they had been there was unknown. Mr. Snow moved in even closer as the mother started taking baby steps backward. She latched onto her children tightly.

"There's no need to be scared. We're not here to hurt you. I bet you are hungry. Can we help you?" Mr. Snow asked.

She began to speak and then paused as she looked around at everyone. "I be Hazel, and this is my youngins, Albert and Becky."

"Howdy," Albert said.

"Mind your manner, gal," Hazel said to her daughter.

"Sorry, Momma. Hi y'all," Becky said.

Mr. Snow introduced everyone to them.

"Momma, you say there ain't no such thang as spacemen," Albert said, looking at the elves.

"There ain't."

"Where then be those green people come from?"

"Don't know, boy," she replied.

All three of the elves giggled.

"Oh, my gracious. I almost forgot to introduce you to three of Santa's best elves," Mr. Snow said.

Emily walked over to Becky and grabbed her hand. "Hi, Becky. Would you like to play?"

"Not until we get something hot to eat. And how about something warm and comfy for all of us to snuggle up in?" Mr. Snow said.

"Mr. Snow, I don't see a diner or my bed around." Jeremy looked around.

"Will you be using that cane, Mr. Snow?" Katie asked.

"OK, everyone. I don't think there's anything he can do for us now. Don't you think he's already helped us enough?" Dean asked.

Mr. Snow looked around at all their faces.

"Maybe there is. Everyone shut your eyes tightly and no peeking. OK?"

Everyone turned their flashlights off and set them down in the hay. Then they covered their eyes with their hands.

"Now, where did I put that cane of mine?" Mr. Snow asked. He felt all around in the hay. "Ouch. Oh, that hurt. Not my funny bone. Boy oh boy. That wasn't so funny to me." He was bumping into rakes, hoes, and shovels that were hanging up all around the barn. Everyone started to laugh as they listened to him.

"Finally! I found it." He picked his cane up carefully.

Everyone waited patiently with curious thoughts of what Mr. Snow would surprise them with this time. He began to say a prayer, and instantly the barn lit up like the Fourth of July.

"You can open your eyes now."

"Wow!" Emily shouted.

No one could believe their eyes. This was the best surprise of them all. On a table lay a Christmas tablecloth and lots of delicious food. There were both hot and cold dishes, drinks, and all the most scrumptious desserts imaginable, from chocolate chip cookies and pudding to silky rich fudge. There was plenty for everyone to sink their teeth into. And in the middle of the barn was a smaller version of Farmer Newton's bonfire.

Around the fire lay several delightfully warm sleeping bags and blankets for everyone to dive into. They lay on thick piles of straw to make them more comfortable. Even though they had not planned on staying for long, Mr. Snow wanted each of them to be full and toasty warm. But that was just like Mr. Snow, so full of surprises and always thinking of others.

"Mr. Snow, you outdid yourself this time," Caroline said.

"We have so much to be thankful for." Mr. Snow smiled.

They all held hands and stood in a circle as Mr. Snow gave thanks. After he was done, all the children ran over and gave him a great big group hug. The children were also great at making Albert and Becky feel so welcome by inviting them to eat with them.

"Come on, Becky. Let's eat," Emily said. She grabbed her hand and led her over to the table.

"Come on, Albert," Jeremy said.

"Momma, can I?"

He and Becky looked at their mom, hoping she would say yes, and she did. Albert and Becky loaded their plates with one of everything. Dessert was the first thing they piled on. After they all fixed their plates, they found a nice spot around the fire where they could enjoy their meal and get acquainted with their new friends.

"Jeremy, that be a cool coat. I wish I got one. Momma found this used one I got on," Albert said as he looked down at his coat.

"Thank you, Albert. This was a Christmas gift from last year. There

is nothing wrong with the coat you are wearing. It looks pretty cool to me," Jeremy said.

After everyone ate more than enough food to feed a neighborhood, some of the children took some much-needed naps. The men got a little sleep too. They knew they would be spending the rest of the night searching for Jonathan. Even little Wanda the workaholic found a nice soft spot in the hay. She lay on her back with her cute little feet sticking up and the soft whisper of a snore under her breath. If they looked close enough, they could even see Mr. Snow dozing off. It was quiet and peaceful, but that didn't last long.

CHAPTER 20

THE BARN DOORS SLAMMED OPEN. Standing there was the army, navy, or air force, or was it the marines? It was four of them dressed in fatigues. They weren't camouflaged in the barn, with all eyes watching their every move. No one said a word as the four men moved slowly toward their group. They all seemed to be fairly young men with guns hanging from their shoulders. One of them was carrying a bundle in his arms. But what was it? It was a big object wrapped up in blankets in a mummy type fashion.

One of their voices hollered out, "Honey, we're home!"

"Kevin!" Caroline hollered. She ran over to greet her son with open arms.

"What's up?" Joshua said.

Joshua was Caroline's grandson. He never had much to say. Probably because he was just too cool for words. All the children thought so, anyway. Maybe it was all the tattoos that covered his body like paintings in a famous art museum. Whenever he was around, the children made him show off his artistic drawings. Following behind them were two of Kevin's closest friends, who he hunted with every year. As he came closer, they realized the large bundle in his arms was Jonathan. The boy lay limp and listless his clothes soaking wet. Michelle dropped her untouched plate of food, ran over to him, and hugged him tightly.

"Jonathan, are you OK?" she asked.

"Mom, I'm just fine. Uncle Kevin rescued me from an avalanche," he assured her. He was having a hard time talking with his severely chapped lips and very dry throat. Every so often, he lifted his hand up and wiped his nose. "I was trapped under snow."

"*Shh*. Don't say a word. Just rest," Michelle said.

Kevin laid him down next to Wanda and covered him up with a couple of blankets. It was funny how she was able to sleep with all the noise going on.

Jonathan glanced at Clarissa, Tiffany, and then Wanda and then took another look. "I believe I'm having a dream. Is anyone else seeing little green people?"

Everyone laughed. Mr. Snow explained what had happened, and that was when Jonathan understood everything.

"Would you boys care for something good to eat?" Caroline asked.

"That sounds wonderful. We could smell the delicious food a mile away." Kevin smiled.

"Cool," Joshua answered as he walked toward the table.

Little Becky walked over to Kevin and tugged at his oversized wet fatigues. "Mister, I be Becky." She smiled.

"Is that so?" Kevin asked. He stooped down and looked into her sad eyes.

"You don't know, but we be homeless."

"You mustn't say that, gal," Hazel demanded.

"Is that so?" Kevin said. He stood up, unsure what to say. He hesitated for a moment. "I think I may have something for you, Becky."

Even though he seemed really tough on the outside, he was like a child himself, always understanding children when others did not. He walked out of the barn and returned with the cutest blackest fluff ball in his arms. It looked like a big hair ball. It turned its little head around, and she could see its coal-black eyes shining.

Kevin knelt down beside Becky. "Becky, do you know what this is?"

"I know, Uncle Kevin," Sarah said excitedly.

"That's great, but why don't we let Becky answer this one."

"A porcupine?" Becky hesitated.

"Well, that's close." Kevin chuckled.

"He's a baby bear cub with no home. We found him wandering

around in the woods near the cave, hungry and alone. So we picked up this cute little guy and brought him with us. Can you take care of him for the night and we can decide what to do with him in the morning? I thought that since you don't have a home and he doesn't either, maybe you could take care of each other for the time being. Maybe you could come up with a great name for him."

"How be Little Blacky?" Becky smiled.

"That's a wonderful name," Kevin said.

He handed her the cub, and they took to one another right away. They were like old friends that had just been reunited after years of being apart. All the children raced over, excited to see the cub. Becky stuck right by it just like a mother would.

"Young lady, look what I have," Mr. Snow said. He handed her a bottle with milk in it.

"Mr. Snow, I guess that just happened to be sitting around waiting for a cute little bear cub." Caroline laughed.

Mr. Snow slid over to Kevin. "You did a fine thing with the bear cub. Did you see her face light up when you handed it to her?"

"I felt it was the right thing to do."

"It's amazing how things can change some people when they feel needed, and you made that happen." Mr. Snow reached over and gave him the warmest handshake.

"I couldn't leave him alone with no one to take care of him. I'm sure his mom and dad were seen by a hunter or two."

"Anyone else wouldn't have given it a second thought. They would have left him behind to fend for himself and fight off all the ferocious animals in the wild," Mr. Snow said.

"Come Christmas morning we will have to find a refuge for the little guy." He smiled.

Mr. Snow leaned over and whispered in Kevin's ear, "Tell me. How did you find Jonathan?"

"Well, me and the guys were out hunting, just like we do every year. It's become a tradition among us to go hunting before Christmas. Anyhow, we decided to head back to the house because we weren't having much luck and it was just too windy and cold. As we headed back to the house, I don't know what happened, but something kept tugging at me to take a path we normally don't take back. There was a force pulling at me to take another route, so we took the long way around instead of the short way. Once we made it as far as the old cave, we felt the ground shake. We saw all the snow coming down around us. As we approached a large hill, we noticed something sticking out from under a pile of snow. We realized someone was trapped under it. We quickly dug with our hands and then realized it was Jonathan." He stopped talking for a moment, took a sip of a hot tea, and quickly went back over the events in his mind.

"Then what happened?" Mr. Snow asked curiously.

"He was unconscious but still breathing. I picked him up and brought him to the barn to warm him up with a fire. Before we got here, a miracle took place. That's the only thing that could have happened. He woke up and was feeling fine. None of us could believe he had survived after being completely covered by the force and weight of the snow."

"That's an amazing story, Kevin. It was almost like God was telling you to take a path because you would be rescuing your nephew," Mr. Snow said. "Hey, everyone! Because of Kevin saving Jonathan, this world is a better place with him and Jonathon in it. I would like to propose a toast for what he did."

He held up his hot cocoa. "Let me see those glasses. Hold them up. OK, children, you also need to hold up your glasses. Get them up there so I can see them."

The children without drinks quickly ran over to the table and filled their cups with whatever they could find. They weren't about to miss out on being a part of the toast.

"Kevin, you rock. Three cheers for Kevin. Hip hip hooray! Hip hip hooray!" Mr. Snow hollered. Then he spun around in a circle, got a daydreamy look on his face, and began to sing a quaint little song: "I get ideas. I get ideas. *Boom chaka laka.*"

Clarissa grabbed Tiffany's hands, and they started dancing to Mr. Snow's little tune. Everyone looked at him strangely and began to laugh.

"Mr. Snow, what's your idea, your idea?" Jeremy sang.

"Why don't we spend the night here instead of going back to the house? We have plenty of food and warm blankets, and more importantly, everyone is safe and sound. That is if you don't mind spending Christmas Eve with a silly snowman."

"Oh yes! Daddy, please, can we?" Sarah smiled.

All the children ran over to persuade their parents to say yes to Mr. Snow's idea. The parents did. How could they possibly turn down an opportunity to spend Christmas Eve with one of the coolest dudes around?

"What about Santa Clause?" Shelby asked.

"Santa will find us anywhere. Even if we are in the boondocks." Sarah smiled.

"If Santa finds us here, that's fine, and if he doesn't, that's OK too. Christmas is about one thing, and we all know what that is," Caroline said.

"We don't need presents to have a wonderful Christmas," Jeremy said.

"Well, Farmer Newton, we have our smaller version of your bonfire, and we do have marshmallows to roast. All that's missing is some Christmas carols, stories, and a beautiful tree," Mr. Snow said.

"I think we can do something about that." Farmer Newton smiled.

CHAPTER 21

FARMER NEWTON SLOWLY GOT TO his feet, limped over to the barn doors, pushed them open with his cane, and looked out into the darkness.

"This sure looks like the perfect evening to hunt for a Christmas tree."

All the children gathered around Farmer Newton and Mr. Snow.

Emily walked over to Hazel and looked at her for a minute. "Could Albert and Becky go?"

"Momma, please. We ain't got a tree before," Albert said.

"It sounds like a lot of fun. Why don't we all go?" Caroline said.

Wanda sat up when she heard this. "Did someone say tree?" She smiled.

They all laughed at how quickly she'd risen when she heard the word *tree*.

"You ought to see how quickly she moves when someone says chocolate." Tiffany chuckled.

As they started out the door, Farmer Newton began singing a beautiful Christmas song: "Oh Christmas tree, oh Christmas tree, how lovely are your branches ..."

Everyone quickly joined in singing and turned on their flashlights. They continued singing through the woods as they eagerly searched for the perfect tree. They searched high and low, here and there, but they couldn't agree upon a tree. When someone picked out one, there was always someone who didn't like it. Farmer Newton was beginning to think they would never find the perfect one, but just as they were considering going back to the barn, they saw it. It had to be the most beautiful tree around. There it stood—tall, slender, and all by itself.

"It's so lonely looking, Daddy. Can we get that one?" Emily begged.

"Yeah, Daddy. That's the one for us," Sarah agreed.

It was funny how everyone had his or her idea of what the perfect Christmas tree looked like. Some thought it should be tall and thin, whereas others liked the short fat ones. But everyone agreed on this tree. Perhaps it was a magical tree, just like Mr. Snow's cane that had led them to it. Mr. Snow cupped his hand around his ear.

"Yes, I do believe it's talking to us. Does anyone hear what it's saying?"

"Mr. Snow, you're silly. Trees don't talk." Sarah giggled.

"Well, you're wrong, little lady, because this one does. *Shh*. Listen really closely and you can hear what it's saying."

"OK, Mr. Snow. What's it saying?" Jeremy asked.

"It's saying, 'Ooh, ooh, please pick me. I'm the prettiest tree in the whole darn woods. I would love someone to dress me up. Look at me. Aren't I a sight with no decorations. Please just cut me down and take me home.'" Mr. Snow laughed out loud.

"You are without a doubt the funniest snowman alive," Jeremy said.

"Could it be because I'm the only snowman here?" Mr. Snow looked around as if searching for any other snowmen that may be around.

"Mr. Snow, will you do the honors of cutting down our tree?" Farmer Newton handed him an ax.

"I'd be honored to, sir." He smiled.

Chop, chop, chop went the ax.

"Timber!" Clarissa yelled.

"Timber!" Wanda yelled.

The children followed their lead. "Timber!" they all yelled.

Thump went the tree as it hit the ground. Before Mr. Snow was able to pick it up, there was a loud screeching sound. It sounded like an animal in pain. Many of the children covered their ears because it was so loud.

Something shot out from under the tree and over to where the elves were standing. It was trying to escape without harm, but because there was so little light, they couldn't tell what it was.

Emily wrapped both arms around her Dad's waist.

"What in the world is that?" Caroline asked.

"*Ahh!* It's after me, and it's gonna eat me right up!" Clarissa yelled.

Clarissa was running around. Behind her was a baby squirrel and Wanda following closely behind them. Everywhere Clarissa ran, the squirrel ran. It was like watching a silly cartoon. Oh how everyone enjoyed the unexpected excitement.

"Come here, ya little nut!" Floyd, the baby squirrel, shouted. "My mom told me that we eat nuts. You sure are a plump juicy one, and I'm starved!"

Sally, Floyd's mom, struggled to get out from under a branch that was lying on her. "Floyd, what are you doing now?" she asked.

"I'm hungry, Mom, and I'm chasin' me a fat nut."

"Son, haven't you listened to a word I've been telling you?"

"I think so," he replied.

"If you don't listen to me, how will you be able to go out into the world and have a family of your own?"

"Who knows?"

"You sure can be hardheaded sometimes."

Floyd stopped for a moment and tried to listen to what she said, but with all the excitement, it was hard to concentrate. So just like all the other times, he looked around and hummed a song he made up in his little brain.

"Mom, what are those little green creatures if they aren't nuts?"

"I have no idea, son. Come on and let's find another home," Sally instructed.

They both scurried away, looking for a home no one would cut down.

"*Whew*, they're finally leaving me the heck alone," Clarissa said as she wiped the sweat from her brow.

Wanda didn't repeat Clarissa this time. Sometime during the running around, Wanda had fallen asleep in the snow. Or maybe it was from all the food she had eaten earlier. The only thing sticking out of the snow were her rollie pollie, chubby feet. Mr. Snow gently shook her to wake her from her nap.

"Wanda, it's Mr. Snow. Wake up. Everything is OK. The squirrels have left, and we are free from all the dangerous wicked squirrels of the world." He laughed.

"I was just doing what Clarissa was doing," Wanda said glancing Clarissa's direction. "I was just trying to get a little sleepy peepy. That's all. You know what I'm talking about?" she asked.

Mr. Snow took her hand, helped her to her feet, and then brushed the snow from her clothes. "Funny, but I don't remember Clarissa sleeping." He laughed again.

Mr. Snow carefully picked up the tree so he wouldn't break any of the perfectly shaped limbs. On the way back to the barn, they talked and laughed among themselves, mostly about the silly incident with Clarissa and the crazy squirrel. Once they got back to the barn, the men immediately threw some wood on the bed of coals that lay glowing. Mr. Snow set up the tree in a location where everyone could enjoy its beauty.

"Now that it's up, Mr. Snow, what should we decorate it with?" Jeremy asked.

"I'm sure we can think of something, my boy." Farmer Newton smiled.

Sarah inched her way over to the tree, took off her gloves, and placed them on a low hanging branch. She looked around at everyone, hoping they liked her decorating idea.

"See, Daddy. It's just like the mitten tree at school." She smiled.

"My my, what a beautiful mitten tree it is. How about hanging my hand warmers on your lovely tree, missy?" he asked, removing them from his cold hands and handing them to her. "Don't forget my scarf," he added as he fished it out from under all the layers of his clothing.

"Sure, Daddy."

All the children went over and placed their hats, gloves, scarves, and whatever else they thought would make it lovelier onto the tree.

"Momma, Becky and me just have gloves with holes. They won't look so pretty," Albert said.

Mr. Snow quickly spoke up before Hazel could reply. "That's quite all right. The holes make them unique. They are special just like you and Becky are."

"OK. If you think it be OK." Albert smiled.

Becky slowly made her way over to the tree, picked out a bare spot where nothing was hanging, and then placed her gloves on it in a perfect fashion.

"Now, doesn't that make the tree look lovelier?" Mr. Snow asked.

Albert gave Mr. Snow a smile of pride.

"Where is the star for the top?" Sarah asked.

"Yeah. It sure won't feel like a Christmas tree without a star on the top," Jeremy agreed.

"I guess this year we will have to do without a star. I'm so sorry," Dean said.

"Oh, Daddy. Each year you hold me up and let me put it on the top. It just won't be the same," Sarah said sadly.

"What if you got half your wish?" Mr. Snow asked.

"What do you mean?" Sarah said.

"Oh, sweet angel. I would like to give all of you a star. The only problem is you won't be able to put it on the tree. I will have to."

"Okey dokey." She smiled and clapped her hands in excitement.

This time, without the use of his cane, Mr. Snow placed his hand on the tip-top of the tree. The brilliant glow that illuminated from it was so beautiful. All the colors just like in a rainbow reflected vividly onto the roof of the barn. It was the most exquisite star they'd ever seen.

"*Ahh*," they peacefully said as they gazed upon it.

"How lovely, Mr. Snow," Caroline said.

All the children surrounded Mr. Snow in a big group hug.

"O little town of Bethlehem," Mr. Snow began to sing.

Everyone joined in.

The night lingered on like a dream from which no one wanted to wake. They knew Christmas Eve would consist of a handpicked and uniquely decorated tree, but having everyone back safe and sound was the most important thing. It was then that Mr. Snow really felt a sense of love that penetrated deep to his heart. The love he felt was so strong that it could have picked up the barn and suspended it in the air like Santa's sleigh.

CHAPTER 22

LATER THAT EVENING, AFTER LOTS of laughter and song, they all snuggled up closely together by the fire. Each of the children held sticks with marshmallows dangling over the very toasty fire. They knew the darker they got on the outside, the sweeter the inside would be. Or at least that's what Mr. Snow told them. Mr. Snow told some of the most exciting and funniest Christmas stories that evening. Farmer Newton was usually the one who delighted the children with such fairy tales, but this year he gave Mr. Snow the honor of humoring them. Farmer Newton seemed to enjoy it as much as the children did.

"Enough of make-believe time. Each year we celebrate Christmas usually the same with gifts, food, family, and friends all around us. That's a wonderful thing, but sometimes a lot of us get caught up in the moment and forget what Christmas is truly all about." Mr. Snow hesitated a bit and looked around at all the children. "Do any of you know why we celebrate Christmas every year?" he asked.

"We're celebrating Jesus Christ's birthday." Jeremy smiled.

"Give that fine young man a gold medal for his superb answer. Unfortunately, though, most children just want toys for Christmas. There's absolutely nothing wrong with that. I, too, even get excited about what Santa is going to surprise me with on Christmas morning, but I always remember the truth about Christmas and how it all began. Waaay back in biblical times," Mr. Snow said.

"I know some who count their gifts," Jonathan said.

"Excuse me, mister, but I do recall another person I know and love who counts his gifts," Michelle said.

"Not anymore, Mom. I've learned a lot this year. It doesn't matter if we can't make it back and get our gifts. Because we can celebrate Christmas here together and spread the true joy of Jesus's birth among us. It took me almost not making it through that horrible avalanche to know what life is about. It can't be measured by the amount of money you have or all the fancy clothes and other material things. It's the gift of life that we were given the fine opportunity to appreciate and be thankful for celebrating every day," Jonathan said.

"And … every year," Farmer Newton spoke up.

"Give that young man a silver medal for his superb answer." Mr. Snow smiled.

The proud look on Michelle's face said it all as she snuggled up closer to Jonathan.

Mr. Snow looked around at all the exhausted faces. "On that note … as my good friend Wanda once said, or has often said, how about if we get some sleepy peepy?" Mr. Snow smiled.

He tucked the children in and gave each of them a big kiss followed by a warm hug.

"Good night. Happy dreamland time. And more importantly, don't let the barn bugs bite," Mr. Snow said.

Immediately Shelby sat straight up in her sleeping bag. "Yikes, Daddy. Are barn bugs big?"

"Not too big, sweetie. Now please get some sleep." Dean winked at Mr. Snow.

Mr. Snow bent down to give little Becky the last goodnight kiss.

"What will be dreamland time?" she asked.

He sat down right beside her sleeping bag, pulled it up snugly under her chin, and kissed her on the forehead.

"My dear sweet Becky, dreamland is a place that is far away from here where little people just like you can visit. It's a special place where you go when you're feeling lonely or just want to leave all your troubles behind and enjoy your most special things in the whole wide world."

"I am not sure what ya mean."

"Let me see." Mr. Snow thought and thought. "If I give you

examples, Becky, maybe you will understand better. How about a fluffy kitten or a fuzzy bear like Blacky? A beautiful spring day with the smell of lilacs and other kinds of sweet flowers filling the air. Playing catch with your friend on a warm sunny day. Curling up in front of the TV, watching a funny cartoon and laughing until your tummy hurts. Going to a baseball game with a loved one and eating corn dogs. A trip to the fair and riding on the Ferris wheel just so you can try to find your house or the ant on the ground that resembles your friend. Rolling your pant legs up and wading in the cool clear water found in a stream nearby. If I were a child, any of those would be my favorites, but it's up to you to choose what makes you the happiest."

"That be so nice. Ya suppose I be visit some time?"

"I'm sure you will soon, maybe even tonight. Because you do know that there's no better time than Christmas for all your dreams to come true."

"Night, Mr. Snow."

"Night night, Becky."

Everyone was so tired that they each went out like a light. Except Mr. Snow, who was very much awake. He wanted to keep the fire going through the night so everyone would stay snuggly warm. But first he would need to go outside and cool off a bit. A puddle of water was starting to form below him.

CHAPTER 23

A NEW DAY BROKE, AND SO did Christmas. Sarah was the first to wake up. She sat up in her sleeping bag and rubbed one eye and then the other. She inspected her body, inside the sleeping bag, and under it.

"Goodie. No barn bugs got me last night, Daddy." She smiled.

Becky sat up with a delightful look on her face. It glowed like the star on top of the tree.

"Mr. Snow, I be visit dreamland just like you said. It be all my favorite things too. I even dreamed of a perty little doll."

When he heard her voice, he yawned, stretched, and rubbed his eyes. "I told you it would happen, Becky. Just think, sweetie. It's a trip you can take every night if you want to."

"Everyone wake up. It's Christmas, and it's going to be a nice sunny day!" Jeremy shouted.

A ray of sunlight beamed under the barn door with such brightness, the warmth was felt by everyone inside the barn.

Dean sat up in his sleeping bag and looked over at Sarah. "Good morning, little lady, and Merry Christmas."

"Merry Christmas to you too, Daddy." She smiled.

He gave her a morning hug and a soft kiss on her forehead. As she turned around to look for Mr. Snow, she saw it. The others saw it too but couldn't believe their eyes. In the middle of the barn stood the most beautifully decorated Christmas tree ever. There were shiny ornaments, homemade gingerbread men (that they could smell), and red-and-white

91

striped candy canes, and underneath it all were the gloves the children had perfectly placed.

"Look, everyone. Santa even left us candy canes and gingerbread men hanging on the tree." Wanda smiled. She was eyeballing the tree and licking her lips.

No one paid any attention to her because all their attention was focused on the tree and what lay beneath it.

"It got to be a trick. There ain't such a thang as Santa," Hazel said.

"There is such a thing as Santa. Look at all the gifts he left us," Emily answered. As she ran over to the tree, she let out a yell that woke up the others who were still asleep. "Santa came! Santa came! Santa came!"

The children were the first to dash over to the tree. Underneath it were oodles and oodles of beautifully decorated presents. They were just like the ones beneath Caroline's tree. Each one had a name on it. The children started picking up one package at a time to see if their names were on them.

"Which ones are ours?" the young girls cheered.

Neither Katie nor Emily were very good at reading.

"Is this one mine?" Katie asked.

"No. That one is Jonathan's," Mr. Snow said as he handed it to the boy, who squeezed and shook it, trying to guess what was inside.

"How about this one?" Emily asked.

"No. That one is Shelby's." Mr. Snow smiled.

Mr. Snow took the liberty of handing out the presents. Santa even left each one of the elves Christmas presents to open.

"Clarissa, Wanda, and Tiffany, these are for you." Mr. Snow smiled.

He handed the girls their gifts with his right hand and held Wanda's in his left. Wanda walked past him, took one of the gingerbread men off the tree, and started to eat it, totally ignoring the fact that he held her gift. He let out a chuckle, which was followed by everyone else's laughter.

"When you're done eating, it will be waiting for you under the tree," he said.

She didn't even acknowledge him. She was too busy eating and daydreaming of being back at Santa's Delights. When Mr. Snow got around to the back of the tree, he picked up two small gifts.

"Albert and Becky, these are yours."

They were still in their sleeping bags. Hazel, Albert, and Becky were the only ones not joining in on the Christmas fun.

"Momma, can we please?" Albert asked anxiously.

"I reckon you can." She gently pushed them toward the tree.

They tore through the gifts so quickly.

"Momma, look. I got a new hat, gloves, and scarf," Becky said excitedly as she put them on. Then she remembered the tree, took them off, and hung them on a branch with pride.

"That be nice, Becky," her mom said.

Albert opened his and received the same as Becky but in different shades of blue. He also hung them on the tree for all to enjoy.

"Hold on a minute, you two. There are still two more gifts for you," Mr. Snow said.

He handed them over. Like the first two gifts, they tore right through them. Becky sat and gazed into the eyes of the most beautiful doll she had ever seen. It was like a trance she was unable to snap out of.

"Oh, Momma. Ain't she so perty?"

"She sure be perty. Just like you." Her mom smiled.

"Thank you, Momma." Her eyes filled with tears, which she quickly wiped away before anyone saw them. "Mr. Snow, she be just like the one in my dream," Becky said.

He smiled because he knew it was the first doll she'd ever had. "*Hmm*, that's funny, but I think she looks a lot like you," he said.

Albert's second gift was a truck, which he was playing with even before he took it out of the box. All the presents had been handed out, including one for Mr. Snow. He was the last one to open his gift, except for Wanda, whose package was still lying beneath the tree. Unlike the children, he took his time opening it. He was careful not to rip the paper so he could save it as a reminder of his wonderful Christmas together with his new friends.

"Mr. Snow, just dive into it!" Jeremy hollered.

"Would you children like to help me?"

They rushed over to him like firemen heading to a fire.

"Whoa. Wait a minute." He chuckled.

They almost knocked him onto his rolling behind. Inside the box were the rest of the things he was missing that the children had been unable to find. They all huddled around him and carefully finished putting him back together. As they were busy doing that, Wanda started opening her present, but the sight of her opening it while continuing to eat her gingerbread man was something to behold.

"Oh chocolate. Yummy." She smiled. She took a huge bite out of her present.

Everyone looked at her, surprised. Santa had given her a forty-pound block of chocolate. It was amazing that she was able to pick it up, considering it was almost as big as her. There she sat among all the Christmas paper, ribbons, and gifts with a forty-pound block of chocolate in one hand and a gingerbread man in the other. She took a bite out of one and then a bite of the other, with a chocolate mustache and sweet beard circling her precious chubby face.

"Mr. Snow, how does it feel to be complete again?" Kevin asked.

"Absolutely snowsational!" He laughed.

"I'm sure." Kevin smiled.

"Well, actually, Kevin, it probably felt as good as when you saved Jonathan."

"Mr. Snow, my momma didn't get a present," Albert interrupted.

It got quiet as everyone looked at Hazel, who was still sitting alone. Well, not completely by herself. She was holding little Blacky and stroking his silky hair. Mr. Snow searched under the tree again but didn't see any more presents.

"That be OK. I don't need nothing. This be the best Christmas ever cause my youngins got plenty."

CHAPTER 24

Instantly, without warning, there was a *jingle, jingle, jingle.* In seconds, Clarissa, Wanda, and Tiffany went running out through the barn doors.

"It's Santa!" they yelled.

Sweet little Wanda didn't even let go of her chocolate for a minute while running to greet him. Everyone else followed close behind them. The children immediately gathered all around the sleigh, and Santa wasn't able to get off.

"OK, children. Let's give Santa a chance to get down from his sleigh." Mr. Snow laughed.

"Thanks for my gifts." Emily smiled.

"Yeah. Thank you, Santa, for everything!" Jonathan hollered.

"Thank you for mine." Jeremy laughed.

"You're welcome. You're all welcome. You've all been such great children this year. Me and Mrs. Claus are both so proud of you."

Albert scooted in closer to Santa and tugged on his red velvet suit. "Santa, Momma ain't got a thing for Christmas," he said. He knew for the first time what it felt like to receive wonderful gifts on Christmas, and he wanted her to share in the same joy and excitement he had experienced.

Santa reached down and raised Albert's chin with his very soft gloved fingers. "Funny you should say that. The truth is that's one of the reasons why I'm here on Christmas morning. You see, your mommy's present was just too big to wrap. I had to tie up some loose ends so she could get it this morning."

Santa looked around but didn't see Hazel. "Albert, where is your mommy?"

"Don't know where she be," he answered.

"I think I know," Mr. Snow said as he slid back through the barn doors.

Sitting there in the same spot as before was Hazel, holding the bear cub. She was still gently stroking it's fur as tears fell down her sad face.

"What's the matter, Hazel? Are you sad because you didn't get a present?" Mr. Snow asked. He slid over to her and helped her to her feet. "You mustn't cry. Everything is going to be OK."

"We all be havin' so much fun with y'all. 'Specially the youngins. When everyone goes home, we be homeless again. I don't ever want it to be ending," she said.

"Let's worry about that later. For now, Santa is here with your gift."

"No way. There ain't such a thang as Santa."

"Yes, there is. And he wants to meet you. Guess what else? He has your gift this morning for you to open."

Mr. Snow took Hazel's hand. She held the cub with her other hand, and together they walked out the door and over to where Santa stood. Her eyes bugged out when she saw Santa. After all the years of not believing in him, there he stood in front of her eyes. Just like everyone had described him. He was so full of life and oh so jolly and warm.

"*Ho ho ho* and Merry Christmas, Hazel," Santa said. He grabbed her and gave her a warm hug. "I'm sorry your gift wasn't under the tree along with the others, but I think it will be worth the wait." Santa chuckled, and his tummy jiggled.

"Merry to you," Hazel answered. She carefully took the package like it was the most precious gift she had ever received. Probably because it was the only one she had ever received. She opened it almost as carefully as Mr. Snow had earlier.

"I be never gotten a gift for." She looked into Santa's loving eyes and then around at everyone else.

Everyone watched with curiosity, knowing what was in the box must be special. Otherwise, Santa wouldn't have made a special trip just for Hazel.

She removed the top of the box and slid the tissue paper back to see what was under it. There lay a photo of a charming gingerbread cottage. Flower boxes packed with blooms of assorted colors adorned the windowsills, fresh white ruffled curtains lined the windows, an American flag hung proudly for all eyes to see, and an old oak tree stood tall with a tire swing to enjoy.

"What this be Santa?" she asked.

"This is a picture of your lovely new home, and these, my dear, are the keys to the front door." Santa took the keys out of the box and dropped them into her hand. "It was just too big for me to carry on the sleigh, and I ran out of wide load signs for the back." He chuckled.

"That's not all. It's completely finished with furniture and lots of nutritious foods to eat. That way, you and the children will get a brand new start with a brand new home. Also, look under the picture and you will find some money for whatever else you or the children may need."

"Oh thank you, Santa." Hazel smiled as she hugged him.

The hug seemed to go on for hours before she let go. Santa looked up into the sky. "I'm not the only one you need to be thanking, Hazel. I had a lot of help, and I believe a prayer or two would do nicely."

"You be right, Santa. I will do that." Hazel laughed.

"You see, Hazel, it's like this: We don't always get what we want when we want it. Sometimes we have to be patient and always remember to believe and trust that things will work out."

"You see, my husband be done left me and the kids when they be wee bitty babies, left me all bills and I just ..."

"No need to explain. I know everything that happened."

"Look at our new house, youngins," Hazel said. She held the picture down for the children to look at it.

"Momma, it's so perty." Becky smiled.

"Momma, it be ours?" Albert asked.

"It sure is. That is a picture of your brand new home to live in. What do you think?" Santa asked.

"Yes, um, it be great, Santa," Albert said.

Hazel gave Santa another hug and a soft kiss on this cheek.

"I bet you believe in Santa now, don't you?" Mr. Snow asked.

"I surely do. I be surely do," she answered.

"It looks like everyone got what they wanted," Mr. Snow said.

Becky walked over to where Kevin was standing. "What about little Blacky?"

Kevin bent down to look into her eyes. "Well, sweetie, I don't know." He looked over at Santa, hoping he had an answer to her question.

"Oh, my gracious, I almost forgot. Clarissa, Wanda, and Tiffany, could you jump up on the sleigh and help Santa?"

"You betcha," Clarissa said.

Santa and the elves hopped up onto the sleigh, where there were two really large gift bags tied with several different shades of ribbon.

"Girls, you get that bag, and I'll get this one," Santa said. He sat little Blacky down on his seat, loosened the top of one bag, and carefully slid it down. The elves opened the other.

"Aww. Are they Little Blacky's mom and dad?" Sarah asked.

"They sure are."

Santa picked up the fluffy baby cub and sat him right next to his mommy. She kissed him with her nose.

"Baby bear, where in the world have you been?" Momma Bear asked.

"Your mother and I have been worried sick. How many times do we have to tell you that bears hibernate in the winter?" Papa Bear asked.

"I a, I a … but, Papa, I wasn't tired. Anyways, I wanted to play with my friends out in the woods. Specially my best friend, Floyd. Do you remember him?"

"Yes, we know him. We know him well. He's always getting into trouble," Papa Bear said.

"Yep, that's him." Blacky chuckled.

"Kevin, there be go my best friend ever. I be missin' him already," Becky said. Her eyes began to fill with tears. She took off running with all her might over to the baby bear, quickly knelt down by his side, and gave him the biggest bear hug ever.

"Becky, it was nice of you to take good care of him for the time, but now it's time for him to go home." Kevin smiled.

Kevin reached down to pick Becky up and comfort her. Little

Blacky turned around to look at Becky one last time. It was as though he'd understood everything she had said. Everyone waved goodbye as they slowly slipped deeper and deeper into the woods.

"I love happy endings." Wanda giggled.

"Me too," Farmer Newton agreed.

"I'm just curious about something. Isn't anyone wondering how they were tame? They didn't attack us and were like old friends," Caroline asked.

"I betcha it was Mr. Snow's cane again." Jeremy smiled.

CHAPTER 25

"WELL, MY GOOD FRIEND MR. Snow, it's time for us to say goodbye," Santa said.

Mr. Snow looked around at all the long faces.

"Please don't go. We'll miss you," Sarah said.

Mr. Snow bent down, and all the children gathered around him.

"When my dear friend gave me some time off for rest and relaxation, I never thought this would be the best Christmas I've ever had. I will never ever forget our precious time together and getting to know all of you. But now it's time for us to go home and prepare for Christmas next year." Mr. Snow smiled.

"Clarissa, Wanda, and Tiffany, please hook up the sleigh and let's get going," Santa instructed.

"OK, Santa," the elves harmonized.

"Come on, girls. Let's get busy. We're going back to the workshop," Clarissa said.

They all said their long goodbyes.

"Hazel, how about we drop you and the children off at your new home that's waiting for you." Santa smiled.

Hazel and the children climbed aboard the sleigh with excitement, knowing their new home was waiting for them. Becky and Albert were just as excited to be riding on Santa's sleigh as they were to see their new home.

"Wait a minute. Albert, I didn't give you my present." Jeremy smiled. He took off his coat and then carefully handed it to Albert. "This is for

101

you. I'm sure you could use it more than I can. Besides, it looks better on you than me."

Albert quickly put on the warm coat as though it was his only prize possession. "Oh gosh. I be so happy. What should I call ya?"

"How about you call me friend for starters?"

"I ain't never had a friend before."

"Well, you have one now. I know just where to find you." Jeremy smiled.

They gave one another a short buddy hug. Not one that girls give each other, the touchy-feely, lovey-dovey kind, but one a young man would give his dear friend, involving a slap on the hand or a high five.

"See you later, chubby little elf gals, and your backup sleigh too." Farmer Newton laughed.

"Take care, Becky." Kevin waved.

"I be missin' you, Kevin."

"I'll be missing you too."

It was at that moment that Becky realized everything he had done for her, all the kindness he had shown her, and the way he had made her feel so needed. She hopped off the sleigh, ran over to him and gave him a super hug and a sweet kiss on the cheek.

"Well, I have to say this was a superbly wonderful Christmas," Farmer Newton said.

"Indeed it was." Caroline smiled.

"But it's not over yet." Jeremy smiled.

He reached down and picked up a handful of snow, formed a perfectly round ball, and then threw it at Dean. It landed right smack on his stomach. Even with all the layers of clothing, it stung him almost as bad as a bee sting. All those years of baseball games and practicing his pitching with his dad had finally paid off. Jeremy would sometimes daydream of the big trophy with his name engraved on the front that he would win. How the gold on it would shine as it was proudly displayed on his dresser for all his friends to envy. Or perhaps of him standing on the pitcher's mound while being watched on national TV by millions and all the many cheers that would ring out from the grandstand.

"Hmm. If it's a snowball fight you want, that's what you will have!" Mr. Snow shouted.

Farmer Newton went along with the fun and spoke just like a sportscaster at a baseball game. He loved children so much, which made it easy for him to use his incredible childlike imagination. The children enjoyed him so much and sometimes forgot he was an adult and not a child.

"Jeremy's the pitcher for the Chillers, and oh what a hot number he is this year with his team being undefeated. They are up against one of the toughest teams in the league, Jonathan's Rockets, and rockets they are zooming through the year with only two losses," Farm Newton shouted.

"Yeah. How about adding a one to that number?" Kevin laughed.

"OK, now quit interrupting the number one sportscaster. He pitches a fastball," Farmer Newton said.

The snowball flew through the air. Farmer Newton hobbled up to the plate and swung at it with his cane, pretending it was a real baseball bat.

"It appears to be a home run. It's going, going, gone. It's clear out of the ballpark," Farmer Newton said. He limped around the make-believe bases with his cane.

The ball was traveling so fast, it was on fire as it zipped by everyone. The wind from the snowball ripped Caroline's second pair of glasses off her face. They flew up into the air and were caught by Mr. Snow. It was funny how they just landed right in his hand as though they belonged to him.

"What a catch that was. It's a shame it wasn't the snowball." Farmer Newton laughed.

Unfortunately, no one caught the snowball, and it hit a tree and then fell apart.

The laughter was so strong as the others bounced off the sleigh and joined in on the fun, including Santa, who wanted to spend ten minutes at his favorite sport of all time. Mr. Snow reached down, squeezed off a piece of his belly, made a snowball, and threw it. It sailed through the air. Kevin ducked, and it hit Wanda smack dab in the face.

She didn't see it coming because she was stretched out in the back of the sleigh fast asleep. Her little feet were stretched straight in the air like she was planning on making a quick getaway if she needed to. Her arms were tucked under her head like a pillow to soften her sleep, and she was snoring softly under her breath. When the snowball hit, she sat up, spit, and coughed up some of the snow that had gone in her mouth and up her nose.

"Are we there yet?" she asked.

"Not yet." Santa laughed.

As quickly as she had woken up, she was back to sleep.

"*Ho ho ho.* Nothing can wake Wanda up and keep her up." Santa chuckled.

"I love you all. Don't forget to write to me. I'm in the Northern Hemisphere book, that is." Mr. Snow laughed.

Back on the sleigh they went as everyone waved goodbye one final time. It was quite possibly the longest goodbye in Christmas history.

You see, not only was Mr. Snow's mysterious cane magical, but he was too. His magic came from a place deep inside him that touched the lives of those around him anywhere he went. The magical place is a place children can slip away to and dream the sweetest dreams and where their imaginations run wild.

They watched with tears as the sleighs glided off into the beautiful blue northern sky, trying to catch one last glimpse of the special friend they'd grown to love. The bells merrily sang from the sleighs until they became a distant echo in time.

ABOUT THE AUTHOR

LAURA STEPHENS COLE WAS INSPIRED by Christmas memories from her childhood, and she enjoys traditional tales that bring inspiration to children. She grew up enthralled by many stories of adventure and has dedicated her life not only to her children, but to others as well.